"A uniquely engaging, provocative, and I daresay fun invitation into the fascinating worlds of the Bible by two master teachers who clearly love what they do and want to share that love with others. It's a gift to teachers and students alike. I can't wait to use it in my own introductory courses."

—Timothy Beal, Florence Harkness Professor of Religion, Case Western Reserve University Author of *The Rise and Fall of the Bible: The Unexpected History of an Accidental Book*

"Kaltner and McKenzie have done it again! As in their earlier *Uncensored Bible*, they have written a lively, insightful, and humorous introduction to the Bible that is sure to keep all readers—especially students—awake, informed, and entertained. In the field of biblical studies, that is no small feat! I enthusiastically recommend *The Back Door Introduction to the Bible* to one and all."

—Brent A. Strawn, associate professor of Old Testament, Emory University

The
Back Door
Introduction
to the **Bible**

JOHN KALTNER AND STEVEN L. MCKENZIE

Created by the publishing team of Anselm Academic.

Cover image royalty free from iStock

Printed in the United States of America

7039

ISBN 978-1-59982-089-7

To Spence and Rebecca Webb Wilson
for their continuing support of Rhodes College

AUTHOR ACKNOWLEDGMENTS

Our thanks to Jerry Ruff and Brad Harmon of Anselm Academic for their help and encouragement in making the idea for this book a reality. Special thanks to Kristi Gudmundson for her work on the maps included in this volume. Finally, we gratefully acknowledge our students at Rhodes, whose engagement and enthusiasm continue to motivate us to become more effective teachers.

PUBLISHER ACKNOWLEDGMENTS

Thank-you to the following individuals who reviewed this work in progress:

James J. Bridges
Georgian Court University, Lakewood, NJ

Paul Peterson
Religious editor, Wilmington, DE

CONTENTS

INTRODUCTION

What Manner of Book Is This?

We finished writing this book at a time when English speakers and Anglophiles the world over were commemorating the four-hundredth anniversary of the King James Bible. In addition to being the largest repository of outdated pronouns and verb forms that thou ever didst lay thine eyes upon, the King James Version (KJV) is arguably the most influential book in the history of the English language. Even those who have never cracked it open are indebted to it for words and phrases that pepper their everyday speech. Expressions like "a fly in the ointment," "the blind leading the blind," "add fuel to the fire," "shout it from the rooftops," and countless others are found in the King James translation. Among the slew of recent books that celebrate the quatercentennial of the KJV is *Begat: The King James Bible and the English Language* by David Crystal, who claims that 257 phrases from the KJV are still with us today.

The hoopla surrounding the KJV's birthday is a reminder of the central role the Bible plays in society and the profound effect it has on people's lives whether they're religious or not. Over the past few years we've been on the lookout for evidence of its cultural influence and have begun to compile a list that catalogs some of the interesting and strange ways the Bible pops up in news reports, entertainment, advertising, and other venues. We'll save the details for some other time, but to give you a little sampling of what we've found we can tell you that the list includes politicians and celebrities quoting the Good Book, comic books based on biblical figures, re-creations of Bible scenes made of Legos, accusations that the Starbucks logo has a biblical connection, Bible rap videos, and online Bible games. That's to say nothing of a rapidly growing cottage industry: boutique Bibles that are pitched to a particular audience. Did you know that there

1

are Bibles out there that target cowboys, truckers, bikers, athletes, firefighters, conservatives, homeless people, James Bond readers, and NASCAR fans?

The Bible is a cultural icon that's often used (and abused) in an unusual manner. But the unusual is not limited to the many ways the Bible is appropriated, exploited, and marketed. Often the text itself is unusual enough, and that's why we've written this book. As ancient literature, the Bible is the product of a world very different from our own. Therefore there's a cultural and chronological disconnect between it and the modern reader that can sometimes leave us feeling dazed and confused. Some of the practices, beliefs, and customs we read about in the pages of the Bible can strike us as downright weird. In addition it's written in a way that reflects the literary genres and conventions of its time, not ours, and that can add to the sense of distance and strangeness we sometimes experience when we enter the biblical world via its texts.

You're about to enter that unusual world in an unusual way. That's why we decided to title this book *The Back Door Introduction to the Bible*. It approaches the biblical literature from a different angle, or rather a set of different angles, by highlighting a number of aspects of the text that are either particularly vexing for modern readers or easily missed and ignored by them. We believe that having a solid understanding of these aspects can go a long way toward bridging the cultural divide between ourselves and the people of the Bible, leading to a better understanding of both how the Bible functioned in its original context and the role it might play in our time.

So if you've ever wondered about what some of the names in the Bible mean or you're curious about what's behind the sexual innuendo of certain passages, this book's for you. If you couldn't care less about such matters we're here to pique your interest and to encourage you to start thinking about this old text in new ways. Who knows what the five-hundredth anniversary of the KJV will be like? We're certain we won't be there. Perhaps by that time there will be Bibles designed for Human/Martian couples or, at the very least, same-sex spouses. But we'll never know. The future remains a mystery, so let's focus on what we have: a text written in the past that we read in the present.

Keepin' It Real

It's a question you see all the time—especially in surveys. The phrasing varies. Sometimes it's about people living or dead. Sometimes it asks only about people from the past. But it amounts to the same question: what one person would you most like to meet, to spend time with, to get to know personally? An online retailer with whom we do business even uses this as a security question for account holders. Our answer? Jesus. Not unique, but easy to remember. Other people are commonly named—religious figures (Muhammed, Buddha, Ghandi, M. L. King), but also world conquerors (Napoleon, Alexander the Great, Cleopatra, even Hitler) and politicians (Jefferson, Churchill, JFK, Teddy Roosevelt), artists (DaVinci, Michelangelo) and celebrities (Elvis, John Lennon). The responses vary according to time and place. In a recent British poll Jesus barely beat out Princess Di for the top spot.

People want to know—want to experience—what Jesus was really like so they can identify with him and feel that he identifies with them. (In a later chapter we'll see the lengths some people have gone to in order to have a Jesus experience.) It's like a study that one of our sociology colleagues here in Memphis did about Elvis. The people she interviewed preferred the old, fat Elvis to the young, flexible one. That's because they identified more closely with the overweight, addicted version. They felt that he was more like them and they more like him. It's often the same with Jesus. Not that he was chubby or a pill popper, but when thinking about spending the day with the flesh-and-blood Jesus people tend to imagine someone they can relate to, someone who understands what they're going through. Such thinking also puts before them a Jesus they could realistically emulate.

On the other hand, spending time with Jesus might be very disorienting. That was more or less the experience of people of Jesus' day. Some of them accused him of being "a glutton and a drunkard, a friend of tax collectors and sinners" (Matt. 11:19; Luke 7:34). They thought he partied too much and spent too much time with the unchurched. He didn't fit their image of a Messiah and a religious leader.

Meeting Jesus might shatter the mental image of him that people have today, an image that often shows up in art as well. You know the common depiction of Jesus in religious art: "a man of sorrows," skinny and sad, maybe with kindness in his eyes but still looking rather depressed and scrawny. And don't forget the halo over his head, the long hair, and the beard. What if Jesus wasn't really like that at all? We don't claim to know what Jesus was like any more than anyone else. But the Bible presents him as more of a whole person than people usually give him credit for. He was sometimes sad, yes, as the shortest verse in the Bible tells us: "Jesus wept" (John 11:35, just two words in Greek as indicated in the KJV). But he also got angry, cursing a fruitless fig tree (Matt. 21:18–19; Mark 11:12–14) and driving merchants from the temple (Matt. 21:12; Mark 11:15; John 2:14–16). He also apparently enjoyed a good party, and if his "camel through the eye of a needle" remark is any indication, he probably had a good sense of humor. He liked to laugh and maybe even tell jokes. In other words, he ran the full gamut of human emotions just like anyone else. In short, Jesus was a real person, and the Bible presents him that way.

Another way that meeting Jesus today could be disorienting relates to his wardrobe and grooming. What if he shaved, got a haircut, put on a suit and tie, or better yet, a pair of jeans and a knit shirt? What would that do to people's image of Jesus? Would it make him any less holy? Would it make him more real? Again we don't claim to know the answers to those questions. They would undoubtedly vary from individual to individual, but just posing the questions shows how our image of Jesus is formed by both the culture in which he lived and our own culture.

There's one more thing about Jesus as a real human that we hesitate to bring up, but it's an important point. Let's do it this way: We have a friend; we'll call him Jack. Jack is fond of pointing out that Jesus not only ate and drank, but also urinated, defecated, and otherwise had the same needs and bodily functions as any other human and took care of those needs as required according to the practices of his day. Now, we don't share Jack's penchant for perversity in pointing this out to people of religious persuasion, but he has a point. Jesus had the same urges and physical needs as any person. If we met him today for coffee, he would likely have to visit the men's room before we left. The Bible doesn't dwell on this aspect of Jesus' life, but it doesn't deny it either. It's part of what it means to be human, and therefore an implied element of the Gospels even though it isn't explicitly mentioned in them.

The Bible itself is a lot like Jesus and the Gospels in this regard. It sometimes addresses aspects of human nature and the world in all their earthiness and messiness. But that doesn't make it any less sacred or holy for some people. It covers the whole kit 'n' caboodle of life, and so it occasionally discusses matters that are usually not brought up in polite company. Another way of putting it is that the Bible can be simultaneously the Word of God and a word about people. Much of what we treat in this book describes the intersection where those two dimensions of the Bible meet.

What's Holy about the Bible?

For the faithful, the Bible is both holy and mundane, divine and human—like Jesus. *Bible* is just the Greek word for books. The Bible is a collection of books. So what makes them or the collection holy? First we should define *holy*. It refers to something sacred or consecrated, something set apart or dedicated for a special religious purpose. It's not the paper or ink or binding that makes the Bible holy for believers but the content.

The story of Jesus constitutes a relatively small part of the Bible. There are many other stories about many other characters: Adam and Eve, Cain and Abel, Abraham and Sarah, Isaac and Rebekah, Jacob and Esau, Joseph, Moses, Joshua, Samson, David, Solomon, Job, Daniel, Peter, and Paul, just to name a very few. And if the Bible acknowledges the humanity of Jesus, how much more does it underscore the humanity of all these other people. Of course, for the nonreligious the Bible is a collection of stories about ancient people, like the Greeks or Romans, who were fully human and did the things all humans do. Either way, there is a great deal in the Bible that has nothing to do with lofty themes of sacredness and morality but quite a bit to do with human beings in daily life situations.

Take, for instance, the law of Moses. The Bible describes Moses receiving the tablets of the law in a very holy setting. Moses goes up to the top of Mount Sinai alone where the presence of God has settled in the form of a thick cloud accompanied with smoke, fire, and earthquake (Exod. 20). The law he is given includes such riches as the Ten Commandments, a code of ethics that continues to be a basis for Western civilization. But that's just a small portion of the whole thing. If you continue reading in Exodus and Leviticus you find quite a bit that seems much less lofty and much more down to earth—literally. There are laws about marriage and divorce, owning slaves, managing animals, lending money, and planting crops. When you get to Leviticus, there are laws about all sorts of earthy topics like urination, defecation, menstrual periods, and seminal emissions, as well as about diet, haircuts, touching dead bodies, and sexual relationships of all kinds.

While we wouldn't deny that in some sense all life is sacred, it's fair to say that most of these activities would not be called holy today. If we expand our reading to the stories about the saints (meaning "sanctified" or "holy" people) listed earlier, we find murder, adultery, lying, theft—in short, real people doing things that real people do, both beautiful and horrible. It's not like the movies and their stock characters of good guys and bad guys. It's real life with lots of shades of gray. And it's also not like Bible movies where everyone speaks in aphorisms. These were real people, or at least they were envisioned as such. They laughed, cried, told jokes, got angry, had their feelings hurt, schemed, and despaired. And the Bible, far from covering up any of it, sometimes goes into excruciating detail.

Things That Make You Go "Hmmm . . ."

But the Bible doesn't relate its details in English, or according to modern conventions and practices. This is another side of its human nature. The Bible wasn't written in some kind of universal language (Esperanto?) that everyone would be able to read. Nor was it written as some kind of magic text that would immediately transform itself into the reader's native tongue. It was written for ancient audiences using their languages and assuming their worldviews, mores, and social ideas. And the Bible comes without a user's guide, so that modern readers are often left to puzzle over what a particular expression meant or what lay behind a particular custom.

That's where Bible scholars and students come in. Bible scholars are handy because we study the languages and world of the Bible—the ancient Near East, ancient Israel, and the Greco-Roman world—to try to understand the expressions as well as the culture behind its stories. Students (and other close readers) are handy because they aren't laden with the interpretations that have become authoritative among Bible scholars and ministers, so they often ask "ignorant" questions about oddities in the Bible's stories, questions that turn out on further consideration to be brilliant because they point to some dimension of the text that has not fully been explained. At the risk of showing our age, we'll borrow a line from former TV show host and comedian Arsenio Hall, and call the subjects of these questions "things that make you go 'Hmmm. . . .'" (If Arsenio doesn't work for you, try Seinfeld: "What's the deal with . . . ?")

The purpose of this book is to point out some of the things in the Bible that make readers say, "Hmmm . . ." and to try to explain them. Why does that character have multiple wives? What's the deal with that ritual? Who are those people? What does that expression mean? Why does the story keep mentioning that name? Where have I read this before? Who was this stuff written for? We're sure we don't anticipate all such questions, but part of our intent is to help readers pay attention to the details and raise their own questions of the biblical text. Learning the characters and plots of the stories in the Bible is important. But we think that trying to get to the bottom of the "Hmmm . . ." questions can be just as important—sometimes even more so—because those questions often lead to the threads that unravel the story and get at its real intent or significance.

We've arranged the topics in this book to be user-friendly. In addition to dealing with a specific topic, each chapter starts by focusing on a particular part of the Bible for which the topic is especially relevant. Those parts of the Bible are in rough canonical order so that the book can be used as one works through the Bible, for instance in an introductory course. We've adopted a light, informal writing style for this book, partly out of regard for students to lessen the impact of having yet another reading assignment. But we've also done this because we believe that learning about the Bible in its original setting should be fun. In fact, our code name for this book project as we were planning and writing it was the Fun Bible. We've had a lot of fun teaching the Bible to our students over the years, and we've had a lot of fun working on this book. We hope that you enjoy it too. And we hope you learn something from it.

chapter 1
What "Assume" Does

Genre

We all make assumptions about what we're reading, even before we open the first page. Those assumptions have to do with the type or genre of literature we're reading, and they shape our expectations about our reading material and the way we approach it.

Take science fiction for example. You don't approach science fiction the same way as you would, say, a newspaper article. You assume the newspaper article is more or less fact. But you don't expect to find fact in science fiction. This is based on your recognition of different genres. If someone did read science fiction as a news report, they would be very confused or frightened or both. In fact, that's exactly what happened on October 30, 1938, during a radio broadcast presentation of H. G. Wells' science fiction novel *The War of the Worlds*.

Reading the broadcast was Orson Welles, later to become a famous actor and director but a relative unknown at the time. When Welles did Wells he didn't just read the book over the radio, he presented it like a live news report, complete with news flashes and updates. While the broadcast was part of a weekly radio show called *The Mercury Theater on the Air*, and an announcement at the beginning of the program stated that it was an adaptation of the novel, many listeners missed the announcement and panicked, thinking it was the end of the world. Orson Welles was playing with genre, broadcasting science fiction as a news report.

The Bible can be similarly misunderstood. When it comes to the Bible, readers tend to read the whole thing as a history book. In actuality, the Bible is much more varied in genre. Sure there's history. But there's also fiction, poetry, biography, and a host of other genres, some of which differ significantly from those same genres today. That's because the Bible is really a collection of different works of literature rather than a single book. And most of the time, the works in the Bible don't identify their genres. There are exceptions, like some of Jesus' parables. But by and large ancient writers assumed that their readers would recognize the genres without having to spell them out. Modern writers make the same assumption. So J. K. Rowling doesn't feel it necessary to say, "Hey folks, this is fiction" at the start of every Harry Potter novel. She assumes her readers know that.

In this chapter we'll discuss the importance of discerning genre for reading the Bible. We'll begin at the beginning, with the creation stories in Genesis 1–3. Then we'll move on to another famous story: Jonah. And we'll end up by taking a look at the books that tell the story of Jesus in the New Testament: the Gospels. In all three cases we'll suggest that the literary genre is typically misconstrued. We'll show how attention to the contents of these works indicates genres other than straightforward historical narrative, and how perception of these genres reveals these works to be much richer than usually recognized.

Genre and Genesis

The problems that have come from taking Genesis 1 as history are well known. They include the fight over teaching creationism as science in public schools, and museums featuring Adam riding on a brachiosaurus. This isn't science. And it isn't good biblical interpretation either. It's an assumption, one that's not supported by careful reading of the text.

There are quite a few indications that Genesis 1 is not a scientific document. It describes the existence of light and of day and night before sun and moon are created, a scientific impossibility. There is also the presence of vegetation before the creation of the sun, which again is scientifically impossible. Genesis 1:6 refers to the sky as a "dome," implying that the earth is flat. Verse 21 mentions "great sea monsters," a term used elsewhere in the Bible to refer to mythological beings like dragons. When was the last time you saw one of those in a science textbook?

Careful reading of Genesis 1 suggests that it had a very different purpose than a scientific description of the universe's beginning. In fact, the text uses a formula for telling about each day's creation. It goes like this:

God said, "Let there be X."

And there was X / So God made X / And it was so.

God saw that X was good.

God called X "X."

There was evening and morning, day Y.

The formula isn't rigid. There is some flexibility in the individual elements. But there is enough repetition to make clear that the author uses a basic formula for each category of things created.

It is striking, therefore, that on days three and six, the formula is broken. Day three begins with God gathering the waters, thus creating seas and dry land (1:9–10). Verse 10 ends with the notice that "God saw that it was good." Here we expect the "evening and morning" line and the notice that it was the third day. Instead, the pattern begins all over again with "God said, 'Let the earth put forth vegetation . . .'" (1:11). Only after the description of vegetation and another "God saw that it was good" (1:11–12) does the expression "there was evening and there was morning, the third day" occur (1:13).

The same thing happens on day six. God creates the animals and pronounces them "good" (1:24–25). Again we expect the text to declare "evening and morning, the sixth day." But instead God begins a new creation: human beings. And the "evening and morning" refrain doesn't come until after that.

A day-by-day outline of Genesis 1 looks like this:

Day 1: light   Day 4: sun, moon, stars
Day 2: dome (sky)   Day 5: birds, fish
Day 3: seas and dry land,   Day 6: land animals,
    vegetation   humans

Eight categories or installments of creation have been condensed into six days.

The obvious reason for this condensation appears in the first three verses of the next chapter where God, on day seven, rests. These verses belong to the creation account in chapter 1, as is evident from their continuation of the scheme of days. The author has related creation in six days in order to provide an explanation or legitimization for the Sabbath.

This concern to support the keeping of the Sabbath suggests that the creation account in Genesis 1:1–2:3 was probably written by a priest or priests. It provides a powerful theological argument for the Sabbath. Not only is Sabbath engrained in the origin and essence of the universe but even God observed Sabbath at the beginning of the world and integrated it into the order of the universe. To try to read this material as a scientific account is to misconstrue its genre and intent. It is also to rob it of its theological richness.

Another good indication that Genesis 1 isn't a scientific document is the fact that it is followed immediately by another creation story. The second story is the one about Adam and Eve. It begins in the second half of Genesis 2:4 and extends through chapter 3. This account contains a very different order of creation. According to it, the first thing God made was a man (2:7). Then God planted a garden to put the man in (2:8). That's when God made vegetation. Next came animals, made by God in an effort to find a suitable companion for the man (2:18–20). Since no companion was found among the animals, God made a woman (2:21–23).

This second story is completely different from the first one. The difference in creation order can be charted as follows:

Genesis 1:1-2:3	Genesis 2:4-3:24
Day 1 – light	First – the man
Day 2 – dome (sky)	Second – the garden
Day 3 – seas and dry land + vegetation	Third – the animals
Day 4 – sun, moon, stars	Fourth – the woman
Day 5 – birds, fish	
Day 6 – land animals + humans	
Day 7 – Sabbath	

There are also differences in vocabulary and setting. God in Genesis 1 is called "God," while in the second story the name used is "Yahweh God."[1] The first creation account takes place in heaven when God begins to create "the heavens and the earth." The second takes place on earth when Yahweh God makes "the earth and heavens." In Genesis 1 everything is watery at the beginning; in Genesis 2–3 everything is dry. In Genesis 1 God is omniscient and speaks or wills everything into existence, while in Genesis 2–3 God forms things like a potter and creates by trial and error in the search for a companion for the man. In Genesis 2–3 there is a single human pair, while Genesis 1 refers to humankind as a whole.

Careful readers who have observed these differences have long proposed that these two accounts of creation originated from different authors. While tradition assigns the authorship of Genesis to Moses, there is nothing in the book itself that supports this assumption. In fact, careful reading suggests that the book as a whole, just like the first three chapters, is actually a composite of different sources and writers. The same "priestly" work behind Genesis 1 continues to appear sporadically throughout the rest of the book of Genesis. But the different versions have been combined in different ways. In the flood story (Gen. 6–9), for instance, two accounts have been interwoven rather than placed side by side. Thus the instruction to Noah to take one pair of every kind of animal (6:19–20) is followed almost immediately by the command to take seven pairs of (ritually) clean and one pair of unclean animals (7:2–3). There are also different chronologies for the lengths of the flood and the times aboard the ark.

There are different theories about the exact process of composition behind Genesis. One holds that documents that were originally independent were edited together. Another takes the view that a priestly author subsumed and supplemented one or more earlier sources. The point is that Genesis is a complex document, with different theologies and traditions from ancient Israel. Trying to read it as a scientific document or as a straightforward historical report imposes a modern assumption upon it and robs it of its literary and theological wealth.

---

[1] Israel's God had the proper name YHWH. Out of reverence, the vowels were omitted in writing. Scholars reconstruct the name as "Yahweh," probably a form of the verb "to be."

Genre and Jonah

Every now and then a tabloid newspaper runs a report about some fisherman in Norway being swallowed by a whale and living to tell about it. The Norwegian's survival is taken as proof of the story of Jonah in the Bible. The assumption, of course, is that you have to interpret Jonah as history, as opposed to, say, a parable or something like it. There's nothing in the book, however, that states that it has to be read as history. And in fact, there are quite a few indications in the story itself that Jonah was written and intended as something quite different. We suggest—in company with many other scholars—that Jonah is a satire or parody. That is, it's a work that tries to teach a lesson by making fun of something. In this case, the object of ridicule is Jonah and his bigoted attitude.

To begin with, there is a lot of hyperbole or exaggeration in Jonah. The book of Jonah is like Texas: everything's big there. The Hebrew word for *great* or *big* occurs repeatedly, even though this is not so obvious in our English translations, which find a variety of ways of translating this term. There is a great city, Nineveh (1:2; 3:3; 4:11), a great wind (1:4) and a great storm (1:4, 12), great fear (1:16), a great evil (4:1), great joy (4:6), and of course a great fish (1:17). The city of Nineveh is so big that it takes three days to walk straight through it (3:3). Unfortunately, this is a big problem for literalist interpreters of Jonah because the wall of ancient Nineveh was discovered long ago, and it's only about 7.5 miles in circumference, an easy walk of less than half a day. So literalists struggle with this one, proposing that Jonah has in mind the larger environs of the city. Maybe. Or maybe it's just exaggeration. Let's read on.

Jonah reaches Nineveh. He goes a third of the way into the city. He stops and shouts out, "Forty days more, and Nineveh shall be overturned" (3:4). How Jonah breached the language barrier (the Ninevites spoke Assyrian and not Hebrew) isn't explained. Even if they could understand what he was saying, it is not clear why they paid any attention to him, why they believed him, or how they knew what to do. In fact, Jonah's message is pretty cryptic. It might mean that in forty days Nineveh would be destroyed or that it would be "overturned," i.e., changed. The beauty of this kind of ambiguity is that either way Jonah would be right. Add to this that the Ninevites had their own set of gods. They'd probably never heard of Yahweh, much less believed in him. Why should they listen to some guy who happened to get lost in the middle of their city and started shouting? And even if they did believe, how were they supposed to know how to respond? No further instructions are supplied.

The book glosses over all these questions and just proceeds with its story. The Ninevites all repent. Every last one of them. (Exaggeration.) And not just the people. The animals too, by order of the king, repent, dress in sackcloth, fast, and pray (3:7–8). OK, the Pinocchio tale maybe we can swallow, but cats and dogs repenting of their wrongdoings, fasting, and praying? It's a silly idea—and our point is that it was intended to be silly to teach a lesson.

In fact, the silliest part of the story is the way Jonah himself is portrayed. He gets the kind of response that most Israelite prophets only dreamed about: people actually listen and turn to God. Your typical prophet would have been thrilled with this response. Not Jonah. Instead, he is angry at God. Turns out, he wants Nineveh destroyed. That's the reason he ran away in the first place: he knew God was merciful and wouldn't go through with the destruction (4:2). He's so upset he wants God to kill him (4:3). Basically, "If you're going to be nice to these people I hate, life's not worth living; just kill me now."

God, ever patient, tries to use this as a teaching moment. God plants a bush that gives Jonah shade, and Jonah really loves the bush (4:6). Did you get that? The people of the huge city of Nineveh he could care less about. In fact, he wants them destroyed. But this plant he loves. Mixed up priorities, perhaps? When God kills the plant, Jonah is so upset that he again asks God to take his life (4:8–9). "You killed my plant. Life's just not worth living anymore." God tries to reason with Jonah, and the question that ends the book encapsulates its point. Jonah cares about his plant; shouldn't God care about all the people and animals of Nineveh?

The book of Jonah is about prejudice and God's love for all people. It's a ridiculous story, deliberately so. Jonah is a ridiculous character, a man so blinded by his hatred of the Ninevites that he tries to run from God, a man whose priorities are so confused that he values the life of a plant over the lives of thousands of people and animals. The book of Jonah was probably written long after

Nineveh had been destroyed (612 BCE). But it was remembered as the capital of the Assyrians, who had decimated Israel. Perhaps for that reason, the Ninevites are used in the book to represent foreigners. In any case, the story is not really about Nineveh; it's about Jonah. The author uses Jonah as a cartoonish figure in order to show the absurdity of his biases and his xenophobia (hatred of foreigners) in contrast to God's concern for all people, not just Jews. In effect, the story is an elaborate parable.

Trying to read Jonah as history confuses its genre. It's like trying to reading science fiction as news. One risks missing the story's richness and true message because one makes it all about whether a man could really survive in a whale for three days. It's like missing the forest for the trees. Or as God points out to Jonah, like worrying more about a plant than a "great city, in which there are more than a hundred and twenty thousand persons who do not know their right hand from their left, and also many animals" (Jon. 4:11).

Genre and Jesus

Just as there are different versions of creation in the book of Genesis, so there are different versions of Jesus' life in the New Testament. In fact, there are four of them: the Gospels of Matthew, Mark, Luke, and John. The last one, John, is so different that it has long been recognized as being of a quality distinct from the other three, a "spiritual" Gospel whose goal isn't to recount the details of Jesus' life exactly as they happened but to explain the deeper meaning of what he said and did.

But if John is more a theologian than a reporter, why can't the same thing be true of the other three? Again, this is a matter of genre. The New Testament Gospels tell the story of Jesus' life not as historical reporting—intent on recounting the facts as accurately as possible—but to persuade their audiences about the nature of Jesus and Christianity. Even the Gospel of Luke, which begins by telling about the research its author conducted to assure the accuracy of his account (Luke 1:1–4), isn't a historical investigation by modern standards, because Luke relied exclusively on Christian sources, some of which were secondhand. He also states that he wants his reader(s) to know "the truth," which is not exactly the same as saying "the facts" (Luke 1:4).

A nice way to get an introduction to the different perspectives of the Gospels of Matthew, Mark, and Luke is with the Christmas story that kids in churches around the world play out every December. Guess what? The Christmas story isn't actually in any of these so-called Synoptic Gospels. (*Synoptic* comes from two Greek words meaning "with" or "together" and "seeing.") Rather, the churches piece together their pageant from these three Gospels, which actually have surprisingly little in common. The wise men following the star and bringing their gifts are in Matthew. The shepherds, manger scene, and singing angels come from Luke. Matthew doesn't mention an inn at all and even has Jesus born in a house rather than a stable (Matt. 2:11).

The Gospel of Mark has no account of Jesus' birth at all but begins with his baptism. Mark's audience is the hardest to discern. Mark may also be the hardest Gospel to read due to its terse writing style, which typically consists of sentences placed together without connectors. The fancy term for this style is *parataxis*, and it reminds us a little of the stream-of-consciousness of *Catcher in the Rye*. Mark is also probably the earliest of the New Testament Gospels, and it provided the basic outline followed by Matthew and Luke. That's why Matthew's and Luke's birth narratives differ so much. There was no birth narrative in Mark for them to follow, so they each put together their own account from other sources.

We don't really know who wrote any of the Gospels. Most English Bibles entitle them "The Gospel according to Matthew/Mark/Luke/John." But these names and attributions are traditional. The works themselves do not identify their authors. We'll use the traditional names to refer both to the Gospels and their authors, whoever they may have been. The audiences the Gospel authors were trying to persuade were also each unique. Again, the authors don't announce up front who their target audience is or what particular ideas they want to promote. We can only discern those through close reading by noticing the different things they emphasize about Jesus.

Matthew was evidently written for Jews—either Jews who had converted to Christianity or whom Matthew was hoping to convert, or both. A number of textual clues make this evident. Matthew describes Jesus in terms that would appeal to people who were familiar with the Hebrew Bible. The starting point for Matthew is a genealogy that shows Jesus' impeccable Jewish roots, traced all the way back to Abraham. The genealogy also traces Jesus' line through David and his dynasty of kings ruling Judah. This makes the point that Jesus was fit to be the Messiah, since *messiah*, which means "anointed," was a royal title.

Matthew quotes a lot from the Hebrew Bible, trying to connect events in Jesus' life with texts from the Hebrew Bible in order to show Jesus as the fulfillment of prophecies and expectations for his Jewish audience. While this style of interpretation has always been popular (compare Nostradamus), it has had some serious downsides in the history of Christianity. It has contributed to the tendency of Christians to reduce the Hebrew Bible to a mere set of prophecies to be fulfilled in Jesus. It also has fostered an anti-Semitic attitude toward Jews as stubbornly blind to the true meaning of their own scriptures.

We're not blaming all that on Matthew. He didn't invent this kind of interpretation; it was common among rabbis of his day. But sometimes the connections he draws require quite a stretch in what is meant by "fulfillment." For instance, Matthew 2:15 explains that the flight of Joseph and Mary with baby Jesus to Egypt was to fulfill the prophecy: "Out of Egypt I have called my son." This is a quote from Hosea 11:1, but a quick glance at that verse in its original context reveals that it refers to the Exodus from Egypt in the past and is not a prophecy about the future at all. What is more, the reason Joseph takes his family to Egypt is to escape Herod's slaughter of the baby boys in Bethlehem, according to Matthew 2:16. There are no historical records confirming an atrocity of this nature. Matthew deserves the benefit of the doubt. He may be doing something more sophisticated literarily than simple prophecy-fulfillment. This story may be a theological device by which he likens Jesus to Israel or interprets Jesus as the embodiment of ancient Israel's experience as a people—again, something that would appeal to Jewish readers.

Luke's Gospel is the opposite of Matthew's in that Luke's interest is in showing Jesus' appeal to all people and not just to Jews. Like Matthew, Luke supplies a genealogy for Jesus (3:23–38), but Luke's is very different. A few of the names match those in Matthew, but most don't. More significantly, Luke's universal interest is patent in that he begins with Jesus and works backwards all the way to Adam, thus emphasizing Jesus' humanity rather than his Jewishness.

Luke's universal interest has to do not only with race but also with social class and gender. Poor people and women play a special role in Luke. It's no accident that Elizabeth and Mary are the main characters in Luke 1, and Luke lets the reader in on what Mary is thinking and feeling about her special son. Joseph and Mary are among the poor, and Jesus' birth is celebrated by common shepherds in the field.

Another interest of Luke's is suggested in the report that Joseph takes his pregnant wife to Bethlehem to register for the census (Luke 2:1). Like Matthew's reference to Herod's killing of the children in Bethlehem, this census is not confirmed in historical sources. Luke may not have made it up completely. Rather, he misdated a local census that occurred after Jesus' birth and turned it into a worldwide event. Luke's motive may have been ideological. Especially in the companion volume to Luke's Gospel, Acts, there is an effort to show that Christianity is not opposed to the Roman Empire and poses no threat to it. Here, therefore, Joseph is shown obeying a decree from the emperor.

As is apparent even from these brief examples, the Gospels ought not to be confused with the modern genre of biography. What biography would give so little background about the main character? Luke tells one anecdote about when Jesus was 12 (Luke 2:41–52). Apart from that, Luke and Matthew both skip from Jesus' birth to his adulthood, thirty years later (according to Luke 3:23). Neither Mark nor John tells us anything about Jesus' life prior to the beginning of his ministry. So there's no attempt to be comprehensive. Also, as we've seen, the Gospel writers are motivated more by ideological interest than by a desire to be historically precise. As with Genesis and Jonah, it's important to recognize what the writers are doing and what they're not doing so as not to misunderstand them. To expect from them a modern concern for accuracy of historical details or to harmonize them so that they all agree would, once more, rob them of their theological richness both individually and collectively.

chapter

2 Family Values

Tube Families

Let's stroll down Memory Lane with the help of Nick at Night, where family has always been a staple. With the advent of TV in the 1950s came such shows as *The Adventures of Ozzie and Harriet, Leave It to Beaver,* and *Father Knows Best,* gentle sitcoms about idealized white, middle-class suburbanites. In the 1960s, as divorce rates rose in the United States, a spate of programs featured single parents (always due to death rather than divorce, thanks to the censors): *My Three Sons, Family Affair, The Andy Griffith Show,* and *Bonanza,* to name a few. In the 1970s shows such as *All in the Family, The Jeffersons, Maude, Good Times, Family,* and *Eight Is Enough* dealt increasingly with real social issues such as race, class, and gender, and also tackled controversial topics like divorce, abortion, and homosexuality. In the 1980s and 1990s parody took over the airwaves in series like *Married . . . with Children* and *Roseanne.* Parody has continued into the new millennium, with increased emphasis on dysfunctionality in cartoon families such as *The Simpsons* and *Family Guy.*

There's a continuing debate about the extent to which TV programs actually influence American society as opposed to simply reflecting it. In 1992, Vice President Dan Quayle famously criticized *Murphy Brown* for its favorable portrayal of a single mother. Quayle alleged that the program reflected what was wrong with America and asserted the need for fathers in families. His remarks generated a great deal of discussion about what "family values" meant. The phrase was coined in the early 1980s by advocates of a conservative social and political agenda that opposed abortion and homosexuality and promoted things like corporal punishment and the teaching of creationism in public schools.

The 1980s "family values" advocates based their understanding of the term on their reading of the Bible. On one level this makes sense, because it is easy to see how the Bible, or many passages in it, can be interpreted to support this sort of conservative agenda. On another level, though, it is highly ironic, because some of the best-known families in the Bible seem to be much more dysfunctional than any sitcom family TV has ever offered. The reasons for the dysfunctionality in these biblical families differ. Sometimes a behavior we might label dysfunctional is simply due to social practices relating to marriage and family that are very different from our own. At other times, it may stem from the nature or genre of the story and the point the biblical author(s) is trying to make. In this chapter, we'll focus on the book of Genesis, especially the stories of the "patriarchs" (Abraham, Isaac, Jacob, and his sons), for their portraits of marriage and family. We will also look at a few examples from elsewhere in the Bible that deal in different ways with family and where recognizing social practices very different from today's is crucial for understanding the stories.

Threesome and Beyond

A guy's wife asks him to have sex with her maid: probably not a plot line you expect to find in the Bible, but it's there. And the guy is Abraham, one of the biggest biblical heroes of all. The story is in Genesis 16. Abraham is known as Abram here and his wife Sarah is called Sarai. She concocts a plan for him to have sex with her handmaid, Hagar. The reason is to produce a child. This makes the idea a little less crazy than it first sounds. Surrogate motherhood happens in lots of societies, ours included. But then, when the plan works and Hagar gets pregnant, Sarai isn't happy as we might expect. Instead, she's angry. She blames Abram (16:5) and then gets really catty, abusing Hagar to the point that she runs away. What's going on here?

First of all, in the words of James Brown, it's a man's world. (Sorry, ladies.) Abram and Sarai lived in a patriarchal culture in which a woman's primary function and value was to produce children. (Sorry, ladies.) Marriages were contractual arrangements between the fathers of the bride and groom. (Sorry, ladies.) Marriage contracts specified the wife's responsibility to produce an heir. In some cases, they even stated that the wife who cannot produce an heir is required to provide a surrogate who will do so.

While we don't have Abram's and Sarai's marriage contract, we do have contracts from the second millennium BCE (2000–1000) that give us a good idea of the social background of this story and indicate the sort of marriage arrangement such contracts presume. In fact, the whole story of Abram/Abraham and Sarai/Sarah in the Bible is pretty much about the quest for an heir. When Sarai can't bear children, following the custom of her day, she provides a surrogate in the form of her handmaid. When Hagar becomes pregnant, she treats Sarai disdainfully, because by the standard of the day Hagar has proven to be a more valuable woman than Sarai. Sarai blames Abram, because Hagar is now in his possession. Hagar's status, after all, is that of a slave. Abram gives Sarai permission to treat Hagar as she will, resulting in Hagar's abuse and flight.

Not kinky enough for you? Let's try another story in Genesis where this same social background is operative although in quite a different way. After Jacob has defrauded his brother Esau of his father's blessing, Esau's threats against Jacob's life compel him to flee to his mother's brother (Gen. 27:41–45). Uncle Laban hosts Jacob for a month and then proposes that his nephew start earning his keep. Luckily, a job has opened up, working for Laban. The salary negotiation gets interesting. Jacob is young and in love with Cousin Rachel. He agrees to work for Laban for seven years in exchange for Rachel's hand—and the rest of her as well to judge from Genesis 29:21. On his wedding night, though, Laban pulls the old switcheroo, replacing Rachel with her sister Leah, claiming that it is the custom there to marry the older daughter first. Back to the bargaining table. Jacob is forced to work another seven years for Rachel, although the good news is that he marries her a week after Leah (29:21–30).

Now God steps in to even things out. To balance the favoritism that Jacob shows for Rachel, God allows Leah to bear children—four sons—while Rachel has none (29:31–35). Then the story takes off like an Old Testament reality show. Rachel responds by giving her handmaid, Bilhah, to Jacob, just as Sarai did with Hagar. Bilhah has two sons (30:1–8). Leah then reciprocates with her handmaid, Zilpah, who also bears two sons (30:9–13). Leah herself bears two more sons and a daughter with the help of mandrakes, an ancient aphrodisiac and fertility aid (30:14–21). Rachel will ultimately add two more sons for a grand total of twelve sons and one daughter. (The reference to the daughter, Dinah, in 30:21 was probably added in anticipation of the story about her in Genesis 34.)

If you think about it for a minute, it's pretty clear that Rachel's and Leah's use of their handmaids here is very different from Sarai's. The main difference is the rationale behind what they do. Sarai and Abram are motivated by the desire for an heir. Since Sarai cannot provide one, she lends her handmaid. As noted, there are good parallels in marriage contracts from the ancient Near East. Rachel and Leah, however, are motivated by completely different considerations. There is no need for them to use their handmaids to produce an heir. By the time Rachel gives her handmaid to Jacob (Gen. 30:3), Leah has already borne four sons. Rachel is motivated by envy. She uses her handmaid to compete with Leah, who reciprocates by following suit. There are no parallels in extra-biblical sources for the use of handmaids in this kind of competition. That's because this behavior was just as unusual in its ancient setting as it would be today. The rationale for the story, in fact, is to be found not in the real world in some odd social practice of antiquity, but on the literary level in what the story explains etiologically—namely, the origin of the twelve tribes of Israel, each with a son of Jacob as its eponymous ancestor.

In these two episodes, then, we have a genuine practice of ancient society that is used in two very different ways. In the case of Sarai and Abram, the practice appears as it was employed in the ancient world and in the purpose for which it was intended: the production of an heir. In the story of Rachel and Leah, in contrast, the writer in Genesis has borrowed the practice and adapted it for a literary purpose: the etiological explanation of the tribes of Israel. Besides explaining where the tribes of Israel came from and perhaps intertribal relationships, the story also illustrates the importance of family and of understanding your roots, matters that were of special significance to ancient Israelites.

Putting on Heirs

As the story about Abram and Sarai continues, Hagar returns to her mistress at God's instruction (16:7–14). Then, Sarah (her name and Abraham's have been changed in the meantime) herself has a son, Isaac (21:1–7). At a celebration of Isaac's weaning, Sarah sees Ishmael playing (a pun on Isaac's name, which comes from the Hebrew verb meaning "laugh" or "play") and is reminded that Ishmael is the heir. She demands that Abraham cast out Hagar and her son (21:8–10). Being alone in the wilderness would be hazardous if not fatal for Hagar and Ishmael, and Abraham complies only after God assures him that they won't die.

The story raises the question of practices relating to heirs and inheritance. In other words, once you have an heir what do you do with him? What's the big deal about having an heir? What's so great about being one? What if you have more than one? If Sarah is willing to condemn Hagar and Ishmael to exile and potential death just to prevent Ishmael from inheriting, being an heir must be a pretty big deal. As a matter of fact, it's a very big deal in quite a few stories in the Bible. A little later on in Genesis, for example, Jacob will convince his older brother, Esau, to sell his birthright (Gen. 25:29–34) and will cheat him out of his blessing (ch. 27). Then, toward the end of the book, Jacob (renamed "Israel") blesses the sons of Joseph on his deathbed, but crosses his arms so that his right hand is on the head of the younger son, Ephraim, rather than his brother Manasseh. Obviously, there was something pretty important about being the oldest son or being designated heir in that culture.

Like the stories about the handmaids, these stories about inheritance reflect the interplay of both social background and literary creativity. The typical practice of the day was to divide the inheritance among the sons, awarding the oldest son a double portion. Thus, if a man had three sons, at his death his property would be divided into four parts so that the oldest son could receive a double portion. For a wealthy man like Abraham with only two sons, the double portion would be considerable. This may be what troubled Sarah, whose way of dealing with it was to get rid of Ishmael entirely, leaving everything to Isaac. Abraham was troubled by her demand not only because Ishmael was his son as much as Isaac but also because of the injustice in that culture of arbitrarily denying inheritance to one son, and the oldest one at that.

Abraham's reservations notwithstanding, the theme of God's preference for the younger sibling is a literary theme throughout the Bible and the book of Genesis in particular. Isaac, Jacob, Rachel, Joseph, and Ephraim are all examples. This theme also carries theological significance as it is one example of God's concern for the underdogs and disadvantaged in any society. It is often asserted that these stories reflect the ancient belief that the patriarchal blessing carried real power and therefore was crucial for determining a son's future. That may be so, although there is also a literary device associated with the blessing in Genesis. The Hebrew words for birthright (*b'korah*) and blessing (*b'rekah*) are very similar, so that blessing may be a way of punning on and representing the birthright. That is especially the case in the story of Jacob and Esau.

There is yet another literary dimension to the story of the blessing of Ephraim and Manasseh by Jacob (here called Israel). It is again etiological. Ephraim turns out to be a much more important tribe in the history of Israel than Manasseh. Ephraim is the largest of the tribes of Israel and is used in some places in the Bible as a name for the entire country. When Israel blesses the boys, he crosses his arms so that his right hand is on top of Ephraim's head, although Ephraim is the younger son. This explains why Ephraim would become the more important of the two. When Israel explains this (48:19) he refers to Ephraim as a nation, i.e., Israel. The author, therefore, continues the theme of God's favor of the younger sibling by casting Ephraim as the younger brother to Manasseh. But since Ephraim is the more significant tribe in Israel's history, Ephraim is the recipient of the patriarchal blessing in place of his brother. Every underdog has his day; even though he's the runt of the litter, Ephraim is favored by Jacob and God.

All in the Family

What about a man who dies without an heir? There are stories in the Bible that deal with this question. Again, they presuppose a patriarchal society. (Sorry, ladies.) They also presuppose an endogamous society in which marriage takes place within a social unit (tribe, clan, etc.) in order to keep property—especially land—in that unit. These stories reflect the practice of "levirate marriage" (from the Latin word *levir* for "husband's brother"). The practice is detailed in Deuteronomy 25:5–10. It specifies that when a man dies without a son, his brother should marry the widow. The firstborn of their union is to inherit the dead man's property and carry on his line. The practice has a dual purpose. It keeps the property within the clan or tribe, and it makes provision for the widow, who would otherwise be destitute following her husband's death.

The custom of levirate marriage lies behind another of the Bible's colorful stories, this one in Genesis 38. Hang on to your seat; this one's a doozy. It all centers on Judah, the founder of one of the most important tribes: the one David and Jesus will come from. Judah's oldest son, Er, is killed by God because he was evil. Following levirate practice, Er's brother, Onan, marries his widow, Tamar. Onan pretends publicly to carry out his levirate duty, but privately he refuses to father a son that will not legally be his. That is, he has sex with Tamar up to the point of climax and then withdraws, "spilling his semen on the ground" (38:9). God is unhappy with what he does (or doesn't do) and kills him as well. Keep in mind these are the ancestors of the nation of Israel, the good guys. This leaves the levirate duty to the third son, Shelah, who is too young for marriage at the time. As Shelah grows up Judah shows no intention of allowing his son to honor the levirate custom, so Tamar decides to act on her own. Posing as a prostitute, she hooks up with her father-in-law and gets pregnant by him. When her pregnancy is discovered, Judah orders her execution by stoning. But then she produces evidence proving that he is the father. Judah cancels the execution order and confesses, "She is more in the right than I, since I did not give her to my son Shelah" (38:26).

Not exactly the sort of story you expect to find about the family line that will produce David and all the kings of Judah, not to mention Jesus. Its ending is remarkable. Judah thus acknowledges that his failure to follow the levirate custom was at fault for everything that happened. As unsavory as Tamar's actions might seem, the story indicates that she was justified because she was driven to act in this way: she did so in an effort to retain her dignity and purpose as a woman in that society. Score one for the single ladies.

Another story in which levirate marriage figures large is that of Ruth. It begins when a family from Bethlehem moves to the country of Moab to escape famine in Judah. The family consists of a man, Elimelech, his wife, Naomi, and their two sons. The sons both marry Moabite women: Ruth and Orpah. Over the course of ten years, all three of the men die, leaving their wives behind. Naomi decides to return to Bethlehem, and Ruth chooses to accompany her, while Orpah remains behind.

The situation is pretty desperate for the two women who return, Naomi and Ruth. There is no brother-in-law for either of them to marry, so Ruth goes to glean in the fields, foraging for food by picking up grain that reapers have missed. Ruth ends up working in the field of a man named Boaz, who is a relative of Naomi's dead husband. Boaz is kind to Ruth, and gives her special privileges in his field. When she learns of this, Naomi turns matchmaker. She sends Ruth to Boaz with instructions to uncover his feet (care to guess what that means?) while he sleeps it off after a night of celebrating the harvest. Ruth follows Naomi's instructions and tells Boaz, "Spread your cloak over your servant, for you are next-of-kin" (Ruth 3:9).

It is not clear how the levirate marriage practice is being conceived of here. Perhaps the custom changed, and Ruth reflects a time when it had been broadened to include not just brothers-in-law but the closest relative. Or maybe the author of Ruth is exercising creative license in expanding the practice to fit the story. The book also contains some other differences with the law in Deuteronomy. For instance, in Ruth 4:5–8 there does not seem to be the same sense of shame associated with refusing to marry the widow as there is in Deuteronomy. Moreover, the genealogy at the end of the book is traced through Boaz rather than through the dead husbands of Naomi and Ruth, which is in contrast to the entire rationale for levirate marriage. Again, the explanation may be literary—an effort on the author's part to connect the story of Ruth to the line of David. Even if we don't fully comprehend the details, it's clear that the custom of levirate marriage is crucial background information for understanding Ruth, at least to the extent that it highlights Ruth's sense of family loyalty and love for Naomi in seeing to it that she (Naomi) would be provided for.

Travelers and Daughters

If it's dysfunctionality you seek, you need look no further than Genesis 19 and Judges 19. The two stories in these chapters are obviously related. They share the same basic plot. In each case, visitors come to a city and are taken in by one of its residents and offered a place to spend the night. In Genesis 19 the visitors are angels, the host is Lot, and the city is Sodom; in Judges 19 a nameless Levite comes with his concubine to the Benjaminite city of Gibeon, and they are befriended by an elderly man. Later on, the men of the city surround the house and demand that the host surrender his male guest(s) to be gang raped. The host refuses but offers the women inside the house instead (Lot's daughters in one story, the old man's daughter and the Levite's concubine in the other). The men of the city refuse. In Genesis 19, the angels blind them, allowing Lot and his family to escape before the entire city is destroyed. In Judges 19, one of the men—it's not clear which—seizes the concubine and throws her to the men outside, who rape and abuse her all night long. Her death, which the Levite presents as an outrage against him, sparks civil war between Benjamin and the other Israelite tribes.

Of all the disturbing facets to this story, perhaps the most troubling is the way the fathers offer to turn their own daughters over to a crowd of men to be ravaged. While there is no way that this can or should be made acceptable to modern readers, perhaps explaining the social and cultural background can at least help us to understand the point behind such an outrageous offer. We are dealing, first of all, with a time and place that has no Holiday Inns or B & Bs. Travel was a risky proposition, and travelers were dependent on the hospitality of others. This kind of story line may have arisen as a sort of cautionary tale or urban legend about the dangers of travel and especially of urban stopping places. It might also have been intended to illustrate the importance of hospitality as a virtue. As remains the case in the Middle East today, especially among the Bedouin population, being a good host to strangers is a sacred obligation. Then again, as we've already mentioned, this is a patriarchal society. That means not only that men were regarded as more important than women but that men were the owners and guardians of the women in their households—wives and daughters—including their sexuality.

To properly understand the text, the reader also ought to be aware that women were considered proper sexual objects at that time, so that sexual penetration in itself was not a dishonor for them, while for a man to be penetrated was demeaning and humiliating because it meant the loss of his superior status as a man—thus the refusal to surrender the male guest(s) to the mob.

Keeping these social/cultural ingredients in mind, let's take another look at the plot shared by these two chapters. Travelers come into a city. One resident is a good host, who offers them refuge for the night. The host is taking upon himself the responsibility of protecting his guest(s) at all costs—even if it means offering his daughters as a last resort to save the (male) guest. The other citizens, however, are wary of the travelers and want to subjugate them. This is not about sex; the men of the city are not gay. It is about domination, the same kind found in prisons today. It's really about xenophobia, fear of the stranger. The way of dealing with that fear is to subjugate the strangers, to demonstrate dominion over them. A powerful way of doing this to a man is to turn him into a sexual object, a role typically reserved for women in patriarchal societies. When the crowd is denied access to the man in Judges 19, however, they do the next "best" thing: they rape his woman, thereby dishonoring and dominating him by proxy.

The clarification doesn't make this story, in either of its versions, any easier to take. It's still one of—if not the most—disturbing tales in the Bible. Perhaps the most important thing to take away from our treatment of it is that it is a tale that is intimately bound up with the societal values of its time. Therefore, the story cannot be naively picked up and thrown into the modern debate about homosexuality, as it so often is.

So what are these stories doing in the Bible? Modern people would generally agree that the Good Book would be even better without them. The quick answer is that they've been handed down to us, like it or not, like an older brother's winter coat that just doesn't fit right. When the Bible was canonized centuries ago, the view of women that underlies these stories was shared by those who made the call on which writings were worthy of inclusion in the scriptures. They're offensive to our eyes and ears, but such tales serve as an important reminder of the chronological and cultural gap that separates us from their original audiences.

Households and House Churches

The New Testament doesn't have any stories about dysfunctional families. Maybe that's a good thing. But the idea of family is very important in the New Testament. The word the New Testament typically uses for family is "house" or "household." Individual households in the Greco-Roman world consisted of the nuclear family—parents and children—as well as slaves.

The book of Acts relates the conversion of several households to Christianity. The most important of these is that of Cornelius in Acts 10. Cornelius was a Roman soldier, a centurion. This meant that he was a career military man and commanded about one hundred men. Cornelius's significance in the New Testament lies in the fact that he was a Gentile who was very interested in Judaism. He was what Acts calls a "devout man who feared God with all his household" (10:2–3). In other words, Cornelius and his family were interested in adopting Judaism as their religion. They were probably attracted by its monotheism and its moral teachings. But Cornelius wasn't a convert, perhaps because he did not want to undergo circumcision, which was required for full conversion. We think that's totally understandable. Then along came Christianity. To Cornelius and his family it was a version of Judaism that didn't require circumcision: all of the benefits and none of the drawbacks. Cornelius took the plunge without having to go under the knife, along with all his household (11:14).

This was a radical step for Christianity and the developing church. There was a lot of angst in the fledgling church about whether Gentiles could become Christians without converting to Judaism and being circumcised first. That's what Cornelius's case was all about. Actually, according to Acts 8, there was at least one Gentile converted before Cornelius: an Ethiopian official who happened to be a eunuch (8:26–40). But Cornelius was the one who attracted the attention of the early Christian leadership in Jerusalem because Peter was involved. His case was also the one Luke emphasized to show that there was no conflict between Christianity and Rome. In fact, Luke builds this event into the watershed moment in the book of Acts. The conversion of Cornelius and his family occasions a council in Jerusalem, which affirms that Gentiles may become Christians without undergoing circumcision (Acts 15). From that point on, the focus of the book becomes the ministry of Paul and the spread of Christianity to Gentiles in the Roman Empire.

Cornelius's story is one of several in Acts in which conversion to Christianity takes place by households (Acts 16:31; 18:8), suggesting that religion in the Greco-Roman world was often a family affair, just as it is today. It didn't have to be that way, as shown by Paul's discussion of Christians married to non-Christians (1 Cor. 7:10–16). But households seem to have furnished the building blocks of the early church. That's why the description of relationships is built on the family metaphor with God as father (Gal. 3:26; 1 John 3:1) and Christ as the firstborn among brothers and sisters (Rom. 8:29; Gal. 1:2).

The ideal of equality among siblings had social consequences in the growing church. It resisted social differences based on class or wealth. Just imagine the reception a Roman soldier would receive from his colleagues if he became a Christian and started to treat foreign slaves as equals. Christianity did not immediately do away with the institution of slavery, but it certainly undermined it. In a letter to a Christian named Philemon, Paul strongly hints, without directly asking, that he free a slave of his who had left home, possibly as a runaway, and became a Christian in the meantime.

Another reason why the family metaphor is so central to the New Testament is that early churches often were literal families. At least it was within a family setting that people met. There were no church buildings. Houses of worship were just that, houses. There were no pews, no hymnals, no choirs, no family life centers. Heck, when it comes right down to it, there were no Bibles. The New Testament was being written. The letter Paul wrote to the church in a given city presumably circulated among the different house churches, if there were more than one. Those churches may have represented different families and in any case were built of different family units.

In one sense all this is not so different from today. But in another sense, the small size of the house churches and the absence of church buildings and all their embellishments means that the churches in the New Testament were very different institutions from those among us today. The Christian church, like the family, has taken different forms at different times and places as it has interacted with and been influenced by different cultures. But the purpose of the church has remained the same throughout that long history. The families and individuals who have congregated within it haven't always shared the family values of Abraham and other biblical figures, but the church remains the place where people worship the God who spoke to him and Sarah.

Don't Know Much about History

What Is History?

History is what happened in the past, right? Or maybe the study of what happened in the past. How about the interpretation of what happened in the past?

Take a simple history question. General George Armstrong Custer: good guy or bad guy? Sort of depends on your perspective, doesn't it? If you're a Native American, Custer pretty much got what he deserved, and the real hero was Sitting Bull. It's a matter of interpretation. And a history of the events surrounding the battle of Little Big Horn written by a Native American historian is going to look a lot different from one written by, say, Custer's great-great-granddaughter.

Not to mention that a history of the battle written in the 1950s reads a lot differently from one written in 2011. Why is this? Both deal with the same set of events, so why should they be so different? It's possible, of course, that the more recent history had access to sources discovered since the '50s that may have changed the picture. But it's just as possible that both histories rely on the same exact sources. So why the big difference?

One reason is that the United States has changed. Our population has become ethnically more diverse. As a result, we've become more self-critical about our history. Coming off of World War II, we were feeling pretty good about ourselves in the 1950s; saw ourselves as the saviors of the world. Westerns were popular in the '50s. The Cowboys were always the good guys and the Indians the enemies.

The tale "Custer's [Heroic] Last Stand" participated in one of the great myths of this bygone era, when the aggressive expansion of European Americans and the appropriation of Native American lands was ignored or whitewashed. This is not to say that Native Americans did not commit acts of aggressive violence as well. They did. Ain't history complicated?

The fact is that there's no such thing as an objective account of exactly what happened in the past. Sure, events took place; certain specific things happened. But the witnesses and sources of information about a given event differ according to their interests and biases. On top of that, given enough time, legends and myths begin to develop. Sometimes it's hard to separate those from actual occurrences. But that's what historians do, at least in part. They are like detectives. They compare the different sources and witnesses to an event and form a judgment about what really happened. Also, historians are interested not only in what happened in the past but also in the reasons and causes behind past events. Again, that involves interpretation.

History and the Bible

History is big in the Bible. Most of the literature in the Bible either recounts past events and explains the causes for them or draws lessons from the past for the future—sometimes both. So naturally, history figures large in the study of the Bible. This is just like any literature: having an idea about the historical context in which it was produced or about which it's written is important for understanding its message or story. So if you're reading Dickens, it helps to know something about Victorian England; early America for Nathaniel Hawthorne; ancient Greece for Homer. (No, not Simpson. For him you need to know something about Springfield.) Similarly, the more you know about the history of ancient Israel and Judah and their interaction with countries around them, the more you get out of reading the Bible.

On the other hand, sometimes the knowledge of history can complicate the reading of the Bible. Like when the Bible reports some event that seems not to have really happened, or when the Bible's version of history gets some of the details wrong.

In this chapter we will examine both sides of the historical coin. We'll begin by talking about history as a problem for biblical narrative. What do we do when the Bible's account of history just isn't, well, historical? Our starting point will be maybe the most famous or notorious examples of problems relating to biblical history, namely the story of the Exodus from Egypt and the conquest of Canaan. We'll also discuss here the role that archaeology plays in the study of the Bible. Then we'll flip the coin to show how historical considerations and historical background can shed light on the meaning of biblical texts.

A Problem of Epic Proportions

It's one of the most famous stories in the Bible, made all the more so by such stirring epic movies as *The Ten Commandments*. The contest between Charleton Heston and Yul Brynner (aka Moses and Ramses) to see who is the bigger overactor. But we're showing our age. Maybe you're more familiar with *Prince of Egypt*, the Stephen Spielberg cartoon version that focuses on Moses' identity crisis and the inevitable rivalry with his boyhood friend, Ramses, when he (Moses) learns he's really a lowly Hebrew and not a (cue the dramatic music) "prince of Egypt."

Unfortunately, history casts real doubts on whether the Exodus actually happened, at least as the Bible tells it. The problem in a nutshell is that there is simply no clear evidence that such an event ever took place. For one thing, the Bible itself is pretty vague about the details, making it hard to pinpoint when the story is set. For instance, the king of Egypt is simply called "Pharaoh" throughout the story, as though that were a proper name. We know, though, that *pharaoh* was a title. It meant "great house" and came to be used for any king of Egypt the same way that "the White House" is used to refer to the president of the United States.

So which pharaoh was *the* Pharaoh at the time the Exodus is supposed to have happened? Actually, there were three pharaohs (at least) who had roles in this story, according to the Bible. The first was the pharaoh who made Joseph his second-in-command and welcomed his family to Egypt (Gen. 41; 47). Then there was the pharaoh who oppressed the Israelites (Exod. 1:8–2:22). Whether he was the immediate successor of the one who befriended Joseph isn't clear. Finally, there was the pharaoh under whom the story of the Exodus is set (beginning with Exod. 2:23). There is a reference to the Israelites building the city of Ramses (Exod. 1:11), which was the capital of Ramses II. That's where the connection assumed in the movies comes from. But here's where things get tricky. If Ramses was the pharaoh of the oppression, as the statement in Exodus 1:11 would indicate, then his successor, Mer-en-ptah, would have been the pharaoh of the plagues and the Exodus. The problem is that we have a stele (an inscribed monolith) from Mer-en-ptah's fifth year in which he mentions "Israel" as already present in the land of Canaan. According to the Bible, though, the Israelites wandered forty years in the wilderness after leaving Egypt before they entered Canaan. So it's impossible to match the few details the Bible provides with what we know of Egyptian chronology. Of course, there are plenty of theories out there that seek to explain the discrepancies. But they inevitably involve some juggling of dates or details.

The stele of Mer-en-ptah illustrates the problem of the Exodus raised from the side of Egyptian history. We know quite a bit about Ramses and his reign. He lived an extraordinarily long life for his time—well into his 90s—so that his thirteenth son, Mer-en-ptah, was already an old man by the standards of the day when he succeeded him. There are plenty of written records from the reigns of both Ramses and Mer-en-ptah, and there is no reference to the plagues or the Exodus or Moses in any of them. In fact, the Mer-en-ptah stele contains the only mention of Israel in all of extant Egyptian literature.

Now, it may well be, as is often suggested, that "history is written by the winners" and the Egyptians would not have wanted to record events unfavorable to them. However, it is difficult to believe that a series of events as devastating for Egypt as those described in the Bible, including the departure of a third of the estimated population of the country at the time and the death of all the firstborn children, would have completely escaped allusion in Egyptian sources. Furthermore, the Bible itself actually records different versions of the events in the sources combined in the book of Exodus and in Psalms. For instance, Psalms 78:44–51 and 105:28–36 differ, both from each other and from the account in Exodus, with respect to the plagues—different numbers of plagues in a different order, and in some cases different sorts of plagues.

It's not just the Exodus that presents a historical problem. The story of Joseph, which explains how the Israelites came to Egypt, also lacks supporting evidence in Egyptian records. For instance, they contain no mention of Joseph, even though he supposedly became the second most powerful person in Egypt, right behind Pharaoh (again, exactly which pharaoh is not stated). Also, the story of the conquest of Canaan by the invading Israelites after they had spent a generation wandering in the wilderness has historical problems. The stories of Joseph, the Exodus, and the conquest are three parts of one of ancient Israel's foundation traditions. At one point, this tradition competed with the stories of Abraham and Jacob, which appear to have been separate foundation traditions. Later authors and editors combined them into one large, running story. In fact, the story of Joseph may have been written to serve as the link between the patriarchs and the Exodus. It explains how the Israelites came to be in Egypt in order for God, through Moses, to lead them out and back to Canaan.

We have here what would seem to be an unsolvable problem. Our best historical information indicates that the Joseph-Exodus-conquest story didn't happen the way the Bible says it did. Either our understanding of history is wrong or the Bible is wrong.

We should admit up front that our historical records are incomplete. The past doesn't change, but our understanding of it does, because we learn new things about it all the time. Still, it seems unlikely that both ancient sources and modern historians could be so far off in this case as to completely overlook an event of the magnitude of the Exodus. Also, it is fair to say that the writers of the Bible have a vested interest in the story of the Exodus that might have led them to exaggerate their accounts about it or that might have caused the traditions about it to grow exponentially over time.

This leads us to another possibility. We are dealing with false alternatives when we ask whether our understanding of history is wrong or the Bible is wrong—although this is the way the alternatives are usually laid out. We should say, "Either our *understanding* of history is wrong or our *understanding* of the Bible is wrong." As suggested in the first chapter of this book, we must be cautious about the assumptions we are prone to make about the genres represented in the Bible. Not everything in it was written as history. And even history as a genre and a concept may have been understood differently in ancient Israel than it is today. To judge from historical writing in other cultures, the purpose of writing history was not so much to tell precisely what happened in the past as it was to offer an explanation for the present grounded in the past. To explain why things were as they were. Sometimes the explanations involved what we would call "myth" and "legend." Applying this to the Exodus-conquest story, perhaps the biblical writers were less concerned with telling exactly what happened and more interested in drawing lessons from the past or explaining such matters as how different traditions related to one another and how Israel came to be a nation in the land of Canaan.

To offer an illustration of this point from another part of the Bible, consider King Omri of Israel. Likely you've never heard of him. Yet he was probably the most important king of Israel, at least from our perspective on history. He had such an impact that for centuries after his death (he reigned in the ninth century BCE) other countries, notably the Assyrians, referred to the kingdom of Israel as the "house of Omri." One reason you may not have heard of him is that the Bible doesn't spend much ink on him—no more than a dozen verses in 1 Kings 16:17–28—and most of that is made up of standard formulas that the book gives for every king. By contrast, the Bible devotes the rest of that chapter and then six more chapters to Omri's son Ahab. OK, Ahab was an important guy too, but no more than his dad. So why the difference? Two reasons: Jezebel and Elijah. Jezebel was Ahab's wife. But she wasn't Israelite. She was from the Phoenician city of Tyre. The writers of 1 Kings accuse her of trying to spread her religion, the worship of Baal, in Israel. They also present Elijah the prophet as her main opponent. In other words, the writers are far more interested in the religious conflict during Ahab's reign than they are in the historical significance of his father. They are writing history, but it is history with a theological slant. That doesn't make their work illegitimate as history; it simply shows us the angle from which they interpreted and presented it. Remember: all history is interpretation anyway.

In the same way, the perspectives and objectives of the biblical writers recounting the Exodus and conquest stories need to be taken into consideration. Our point here isn't to try to solve the historical problem of the Exodus. We just want to demonstrate that the Exodus is a complex problem of many dimensions both historical and literary. What history shows us in this instance is not that the Bible is "wrong" but that we have not fully appreciated the genre and purpose of the Joseph-Exodus-conquest complex.

The Dirt on Archaeology

Before moving on to discuss other ways that history helps with understanding the Bible, we want to pause for a few remarks on archaeology. Contrary to popular belief, archaeology is not an objective science like, say, chemistry or physics (though there are plenty of variables in these "hard" sciences as well). Guess what? Interpretation is a huge part of archaeology just as it is of history and biblical studies.

The whole approach to archaeology has changed dramatically in the last thirty to forty years. This is due to the influence of archaeological study and practice in the New World, i.e., the Americas. In contrast to the Old World—Greece, Rome, the ancient Near East— where there were texts that could help interpret the artifacts, in the Americas the texts were nonexistent or unreadable. Archaeology had to step it up and learn to extract more information from the material remains apart from written records. Archaeologists accomplished this through greater attention to detail and increased reliance on science. For example, the dirt that had previously been tossed aside at an excavation is now sifted and screened to recover tiny remains such as seeds and rodent bones. These, in turn, yield information about the diet and agricultural habits of the people who lived where the archaeologists are working. These newer methods have caught on quickly and are now commonly used at Old World sites as well as New World ones.

As a result of these newer methods, the field of archaeology has been revolutionized. A new focus has developed on the daily life of common people rather than on the upper classes and elite strata of society. It has become possible to get an idea of the role played by certain segments of the population, such as women. Archaeological excavation has become more detailed and technical. It has learned to gain more from less, so that these days, for instance, only about 10 percent of any given site is dug. This is intentional. Archaeology is by nature a destructive science, so it is designed to leave plenty of evidence for future excavators, who will hopefully be using even more sophisticated methods of analysis. Of course, doing archaeology according to new, scientific methods is also very expensive, so that most projects can't afford to excavate a site in its entirety.

How does all of this relate to the Bible? Well, there are trade-offs. On the one hand, we learn less about the elite groups, such as kings, who are the focus of many of the Bible's narratives. On the other hand, we learn more about the daily life of the common people of ancient Israel and what it was really like for most people to live then and there. Fortunately, archaeology is also able to focus on specific questions, especially with its newer methods. One such question concerns the origins and ethnicity of Israel. What does the material culture reveal about where the people who identified themselves as Israel really came from? The best answer currently available is that they came from within Canaan. The reason that we express this result so tentatively is that archaeology as a discipline and in its results is constantly changing. There is still an enormous amount of work to be done, and an equal amount of excavation work that has already been done that needs to be synthesized and published. Archaeologists aren't the most efficient at getting their work out in published form. In fact, there are estimates that as much as 90 percent of the material excavated in Syria-Palestine (including Israel) remains unpublished. Some of our more snarky Bible scholar colleagues refer to this as archaeology's "dirty little secret." Needless to say, a lot about our understanding of life in ancient Israel could change with access to this archaeological data.

We don't mean to sound overly pessimistic. Archaeology has taught us a lot and no doubt has a lot more to teach us. We draw the best conclusions we can with what archaeology gives us. But it is always worth keeping in mind that those conclusions, however well founded, are subject to change. History and archaeology, as well as study of the Bible, are best conducted with a large dose of humility.

The Helping Hand of History

Despite the problems that history raises for certain texts and stories in the Bible, it is an essential tool for interpretation. Perhaps nowhere in the Hebrew Bible is this clearer than in the case of the "Immanuel oracle" in Isaiah 7. You can see the importance of history to this narrative in the first verse. It is dated, "In the days of Ahaz son of Jotham son of Uzziah, king of Judah." And it goes on to mention two other kings, "King Rezin of Aram and King Pekah son of Remaliah of Israel." The verse sets the stage for the entire chapter by relating that the latter two kings "went up to attack Jerusalem, but could not mount an attack against it."

The episode that this chapter relates is commonly known as the "Syro-Ephraimitic crisis." It was an event that took place in 734 BCE. The *crisis* was for Judah and its king, Ahaz, caused by the attack of Syria and Israel, also known as Ephraim. Here's the cast of characters:

King	Country	Capital	Other Names
Ahaz, son of Jotham	Judah	Jerusalem	House of David
Rezin	Aram/Syria	Damascus	
Pekah, son of Remaliah	Israel	Samaria	Ephraim

There are other details, but that's enough to help us follow the plot of the narrative and to show that it concerns a historical situation. Basically, the city of Jerusalem, where Ahaz sits as king of Judah, was under attack from Syria and Israel. Ahaz and the people of Jerusalem were afraid, or as verse 2 puts it, their hearts "shook as the trees of the forest shake before the wind." Enter the prophet Isaiah. He had a very simple message for Ahaz: relax, don't be afraid. In other words, trust God to resolve this problem. Again, the text puts it this way, "Take heed, be quiet, do not fear, and do not let your heart be faint because of these two smoldering stumps of fire-brands, because of the fierce anger of Rezin and Aram and the son of

Remaliah" (v. 4). Isaiah went on to assert that their plan to remove Ahaz as king and replace him with a figurehead of their choosing was not going to work: "It shall not stand, and it shall not come to pass" (v. 7).

Behind Isaiah's advice was a matter of international politics. He was trying to keep Ahaz from sending for help to the Assyrian king, Tiglath-Pileser III. Isaiah's reasoning was sound. Tiglath-Pileser was going to attack Syria and Israel anyway, all the more since their defenses were diminished by their siege of Jerusalem. Ahaz would have done well to listen to Isaiah, wait out the siege, and come out of the whole thing without any obligation to Assyria.

Isaiah cast his advice as a matter of faith and trust in God on Ahaz's part: "If you do not stand firm in faith, you shall not stand at all" (v. 9). He even offered Ahaz the chance to ask for a sign. Ahaz, for whatever reason, refused. So Isaiah chose his own sign. Isaiah's sign, or rather Yahweh's sign, was really another way of telling Ahaz that he should not be afraid of Syria and Israel.

> Therefore the LORD himself will give you a sign. Look, the young woman is with child and shall bear a son, and shall name him Immanuel. He shall eat curds and honey by the time he knows how to refuse the evil and choose the good. For before the child knows how to refuse the evil and choose the good, the land before whose two kings you are in dread will be deserted. (7:14–16)

The sign referred to a woman who was pregnant—perhaps even Ahaz's or Isaiah's wife. What the sign did was establish a time frame; by the time the son of this pregnant woman became able to "refuse the evil and choose the good," Syria and Israel would be destroyed. Since "refusing the evil and choosing the good" was associated with food, it was likely a reference to weaning. "Curds and honey" were luxury items not available in a siege. So the point was that by the time the child was weaned (2–3 years) the siege would be long over and Syria and Israel no longer a threat to Judah. The sign still demanded faith from Ahaz. The name of the yet-to-be-born child, "Immanuel," meant "God is with us," which was Isaiah's point to Ahaz: trust in God, not in Tiglath-Pileser III.

Centuries later, the author of the Gospel of Matthew reused Isaiah's oracle in reference to Jesus' birth. The main reason for this reuse was the name Immanuel, which seemed so appropriate for Christ. This is an example of the reinterpretation of biblical materials by later biblical authors, which we'll save for discussion in our later chapter, "Recycling." Our point for now is to show how historical background is crucial for understanding what is going on in the passage in Isaiah 7 and for the prophet's message there.

When in Rome . . . Or Not

The New Testament books written by Paul were all originally letters. They get their names from the places where the people he was writing to lived: Rome, Corinth, Galatia, etc. These were all "occasional" or "situational" letters because in them Paul addressed specific occasions or situations being dealt with by the Christians and churches in those places. In 1 Corinthians, for example, Paul responded to a letter from the Corinthian Christians about a whole series of issues they were having. You can tick them off as you read through the letter: divisions, sexual immorality (in the form of a man living with his father's wife), lawsuits among Christians, marriage and sexual relations, food sacrificed to idols, head covering during prayer, the Lord's Supper, spiritual gifts, the return of Christ, and collecting money for famine relief in Jerusalem. We will deal with a couple of these in a chapter on culture. We'll also discuss the focus of Paul's letter to the Galatians in the chapter on race.

The one possible exception—the one letter of Paul that might not be situational—is the Epistle to the Romans, which has sometimes been described as a kind of theological treatise by Paul in which he systematically lays out his understanding of Christianity. It was Romans, for instance, where Martin Luther got his principle of salvation by faith not works that led him to launch a reform movement of the Catholic Church that ultimately resulted in the forming of the Protestant denominations.

While it is true that the situation behind the Epistle to the Romans was broader than it was for other letters, Paul still had a very specific reason for writing the letter, and historical events in the middle of the first century CE provide us with an important clue to his purpose. In the year 49 CE, the Roman emperor Claudius expelled the Jews from the city. The Roman historian Suetonius is our source for this event. He reports that the expulsion was because of turmoil over someone called "Chrestus," by which he probably meant "Christ" (that is, he mistook the unfamiliar Greek word "Christ" for the common Roman name "Chrestus"). There seems to have been a growing conflict between Christians and Jews in the city of Rome— more specifically between Jews who had converted to Christianity and those who had not.

The Jews were banished for five years and returned in 54. By that time, the makeup of the church in Rome had no doubt changed a great deal. Gentile Christians had probably come to outnumber those with Jewish roots. There may have been some tensions between the two groups. We don't know for sure. What is clear is that Paul tried to articulate his own views and his mission "to the Jew first and also to the Greek (i.e., the Gentile)" (1:16), emphasizing God's love for all and the availability of salvation to everyone: "For there is no distinction between Jew and Greek; the same LORD is LORD of all and is generous to all who call on him" (10:12). It has even been suggested that the people in Rome had heard about Paul's harsh words to the Galatians over the issue of Jewish-Gentile relations and were a little skeptical of him. Paul may have been trying to clarify and even soften his language and his image. He wanted to help the Roman Christians avoid tensions and problems over racial differences that had been experienced by other churches and could have been exacerbated by the five-year expulsion of the Jews.

Paul also wanted to make new friends, and that was his other reason for writing. In the final chapter of the book, he sends greetings to the Christians in Rome, mentioning twenty-six of them by name. Judging from those names, some are Jewish, more are Gentiles. Some of these folks were people Paul knew personally from elsewhere; others were friends of friends. But Paul himself had never been to Rome—and he wanted to go, as he stated in 15:23. He intended, in fact, to use Rome as the jumping-off point for his further mission to Spain. He hoped to find a healthy and sympathetic church there that would support his travels further west. We don't know for certain whether Paul ever made it to Spain. The book of Acts ends with him in Rome, so he apparently made it that far. In any case, thanks in part to Suetonius and Roman history, we have a better understanding of the situation that occasioned Paul's writing of this letter.

In sum, history is the stage on which the story of the Bible is played out. Sometimes the set is crucial for understanding the play. Sometimes liberties are taken with the set for artistic purposes relating to a scene's unique perspective or message. In all cases, the set is integral to the production, which can neither take place nor be understood in a vacuum.

4 Culture Shock

When in Rome

Being real men, we love the movie *Jeremiah Johnson*. In that 1972 film, Robert Redford stars as a soldier in the mid-nineteenth century who flees the horrors of war to become a mountain man. Early in his new career, while he is learning his way around his new environment, he offers some ponies he doesn't need to a Native American chief. This is a big mistake. According to the tribe's practice, the chief is obligated to come up with a gift to top Jeremiah's or else have him killed for insulting the chief's honor. Fortunately, the chief comes up with something better—at least in his estimation. He offers Jeremiah his daughter as a wife. The mountain man doesn't want her but doesn't dare refuse.

Likely you've heard about customs like this in other cultures. If you haven't, check out the National Geographic channel. Often, strange customs are associated with religion: the veiling of women, the clothing worn or in some cases not worn by religious officials, foods considered delicacies and eaten on special occasions. A lot of such customs have to do with body markings, piercings, disfigurements, and so on at various stages of life. It may not be politically correct to refer to or even think of such practices as "strange," but it is hard not to do so. Of course, with a little thought and experience, we can also begin to see how odd some of our own customs must appear to people from other cultures. Try explaining slumber parties or the Macy's Thanksgiving Day parade to someone from Nepal.

Because the Bible has become such an integral part of Western culture, it's easy to forget that it comes from cultures that were very different from our own. But some of the practices described in the Bible are just as strange as those on NatGeo. If they don't seem strange, it's only because we are used to reading about them in the Bible, and in some cases, continuing a vestige of the original practice. In this chapter, we will take a look at some of the weird practices in the Bible, starting with one of the strangest: circumcision. The launching point for our discussion will be the laws in the books of Exodus, Leviticus, and Deuteronomy.

Circle of Trust

Circumcision of males means cutting off the foreskin that covers the glans or head of the penis. Say what? You gotta ask, "Why? Whose bright idea was this custom?" The truth is we don't know exactly where and how the practice began. However, there are enough hints to make a pretty good guess.

The Bible mandates circumcision of all male babies on their eighth day of life for ancient Israelites: "On the eighth day the flesh of his foreskin shall be circumcised" (Leviticus 12:3). It traces the custom back to a command given to Abraham in Genesis 17. As children of Abraham, Muslims also follow this practice. In the Bible, circumcision becomes a way of distinguishing the Israelites from other peoples, such as the Philistines, who are constantly referred to as the uncircumcised. Ouch.

Turns out, though, that the circumcised weren't all that exclusive a club. Israelites weren't the only ones or the first ones to practice circumcision. In addition to Arab tribes, the Egyptians also practiced it a long time before Abraham. What's more, the Bible itself is somewhat ambiguous about how it originated. The commands about circumcision in Genesis 17 and Leviticus 12:3 are from the Priestly source or writer (P), which is the latest of the levels of writing in the Pentateuch, probably from the exile (sixth century BCE) and so toward the end of the history covered in the Hebrew Bible. Other allusions to circumcision in the Bible indicate that it was being practiced among the Israelites long before these texts were written. In other words, the practice itself was quite old. Note that the Bible doesn't claim that the practice originated with Abraham, just that its significance for Israelites began with him—and even at that, the story that associates the practice with Abraham dates to a much later era. So again, where did it come from?

There are a couple of other passages in the Bible that suggest that the origins of circumcision among the Israelites were more complicated than a simple command to Abraham. Unfortunately, both of these passages have their own complications. One of them (Exod. 4:24–26) relates one of the strangest episodes in the Bible. Moses is on his way back to Egypt to lead the people out of slavery. His family, consisting of his wife and baby son, is traveling with him. So far so good. But you won't believe what happens next. God meets him and tries to kill him. Say what? Then it gets even weirder. Moses' wife grabs a flint knife, circumcises the boy, and touches the bloody foreskin to Moses' uncircumcised penis. As she does so, she says to Moses, "You are a bridegroom of blood to me." Weird? Definitely. But it works. Her actions placate God, who then leaves Moses alone. The story then repeats, "A bridegroom of blood by circumcision."

At least that's the way we read this bizarre tale. The Hebrew text isn't actually clear on a few points—like who it is, precisely, that God is trying to kill. The text just uses pronouns: "met him" and "tried to kill him." It also doesn't mention Moses' penis exactly. It says that Zipporah, Moses' wife, cut off her son's foreskin and touched "his feet." The word *feet* is a common euphemism for the genitals in the Bible, which would make sense in a passage about circumcision (see chapter 6 in this book). Again it's not clear whose "feet" these are. But if it is a euphemism, the penis being touched would have belonged to Moses since the baby's has just been circumcised. If this interpretation is correct—and it's not unique or original to us—Zipporah performs circumcision by proxy. She circumcises her son and then uses his circumcision to count for Moses by spreading the blood from the child's circumcised foreskin on Moses' uncircumcised penis in order to keep God from killing him.

Still confused? You have every right to be. There's still plenty about this story that boggles the mind. For starters, why is God trying to kill Moses now after spending so much time preparing him for his mission? And what's up with God *trying* to kill Moses? If

God is trying to kill you, aren't you pretty much toast? Also, how does Zipporah know what to do? If you run into God somewhere and he is out to kill your husband, would your first instinct be to grab a knife and slice your boy's man parts? The story screams "etiology!" Specifically, it provides an etiology for circumcision, and the reference to "bridegroom" suggests a connection between the custom and marriage, maybe as a rite of passage for males of marriageable age to make them eligible for marriage. We may even hazard the guess that the story was meant to explain the transfer of the rite of circumcision from males eligible for marriage to newborns. Exactly why it became connected with Moses is hard to say. Maybe it's making the point that Moses, as leader and representative of Israel, really needed to have the sign of God's covenant with Israel on his person.

The other relevant text is Joshua 5:2–9. Here the Israelites are commanded to circumcise themselves before they enter the promised land. The explanation given is that the generation that came out of Egypt and had to wander in the wilderness because it did not trust Yahweh to fulfill his promise also had failed to perform the rite of circumcision upon its children. Hence, the new generation had to perform circumcision upon themselves. There is an interesting connection in this story between circumcision and the promised land. The new generation must circumcise themselves before they can inherit the promise of God to their ancestors to give them the land and make them a great nation. Here circumcision is not a rite of passage but a marker of national and ethnic identity. The "disgrace of Egypt" in verse 9 may allude to a kind of circumcision practiced by Egyptians in which the slit foreskin was allowed to hang free rather than being completely removed. In contrast to this pre-zipper version, the Hebrew custom "rolled away" the foreskin completely (a pun on the name Gilgal, which sounds like *galal*, the Hebrew verb for "roll") to distinguish Israelites from Egyptians.

Based on these texts and on comparative anthropological evidence about how circumcision is practiced elsewhere (check out NatGeo), it seems likely that the custom began as a rite of passage for males of marriageable age. That accounts for the connection with the reproductive organs. It evolved into a sign of ethnic identity for Israelites as the people of Yahweh, even though they were not completely alone in observing it.

A Meaty Matter

Question 1: You send an e-mail to your sister and you want to copy your brother on it. Your brother's address goes on the line marked "cc." Do you know what "cc" stands for and why?

Answer: A "cc" is a "carbon copy," because in the age of typewriters people used carbon paper to make copies of typewritten documents.

Question 2: It's 3:30 a.m. and nothing's on but infomercials. You decide to buy a set of steak knives (only $19.95) and are told to dial the number on the screen. Why "dial"?

Answer: Also in that age, telephones were equipped with dials rather than buttons, so you literally had to dial a number with your finger to make a call.

There are many frozen expressions linked to devices that no one uses any more. The language hangs on to describe the same function now performed in a different way.

That's the way it is with sacrifice. Christians sing about "the blood of the lamb," but few of us have ever offered an animal sacrifice. In fact, the very act of killing an animal is foreign to most of us. We don't live on farms. Our meat comes processed and packaged. We've never slaughtered and butchered an animal for food, much less for sacrifice. In the ancient world, though, animal sacrifice was commonplace. It was part of a larger system of religious thought and practice. That system is assumed in the Bible. So if we want to understand the theology and religious perspective of the Bible, we have to get some sense of how sacrifice worked.

The attention and detail that the Hebrew Bible devotes to sacrifice and how to do it shows just how important it was in ancient Israel. There's a whole book—Leviticus, named after the priestly tribe of Levi—that's devoted to regulations relating to the duties of priests. Sacrifice is a major part of those duties. The first seven chapters of Leviticus give specific rules for sacrifice. Then in chapter 17 a new section of Leviticus begins what most scholars see as a distinct and later addition, dubbed the "Holiness Code." It also begins with instructions about sacrifice and offers an overview that is helpful for understanding some of the ideology behind the practice.

Ancient Israel practiced different kinds of sacrifices. Sacrifices of "well-being" or "peace offerings" are covered in Leviticus 3; 7:11–34; and 17. Such sacrifices had broad application and could be offered for a variety of reasons, including giving thanks, fulfilling a vow, or simply as a voluntary sacrifice to God. It was also the only kind of sacrifice in which laypersons, i.e., nonpriests, fully participated. This means two things. First, perhaps because of the involvement of nonspecialists, the passages about sacrifices of well-being go into detail about the principles behind sacrifice—the assumption being that laypersons would need instruction in such principles. That's why we'll focus on this type of sacrifice. Second, "full participation" in this case means that the person who brought the sacrifice consumed it. In fact, sacrifice and the eating of meat were closely tied together.

Leviticus 17 outlaws the slaughter of domesticated animals outside of sacrifice at the tabernacle. So if you wanted a steak or lamb chops, you had to bring the animal to the tabernacle for the priests to slaughter. The blood would be drained and sprinkled by the priest upon the altar. Part of the animal, mainly the entrails and the fat covering them, was burned as a sacrifice to God. Part would go to the priest as payment. The rest was yours to eat. Steak and chops.

The reasons for these different steps are explained in Leviticus and elsewhere in the Bible in material written by priests. The conceptual principles undergirding sacrifice begin with the Noah story in Genesis. Blood is considered the source of life. It's holy and is never to be eaten (Gen. 9:4; Lev. 17:11–12). Shedding blood or taking a life is God's prerogative as the giver of all life. So the basic rule is that killing is something humans are not supposed to do. Shedding human blood is wrong (Gen. 9:5–6).

Still, God makes the rules so God makes allowances. Beginning with Noah, humans can slaughter animals for food (Gen. 9:3). Then, under Moses in the wilderness, God starts requiring compensation for the slaughter of domesticated animals. The compensation is in the form of sacrifice of what was considered the best parts of those animals. To slaughter an animal without sacrificing part of it to God is bloodshed and tantamount to murder (Lev. 17:4). That's because God was not compensated for the loss of life. In some ancient texts the gods are even understood to eat the sacrifices. And some Bible passages contain a remnant of this in their language and imagery of

God being pleased by the smell of the sacrifice (Gen. 8:21; Lev. 1:9; 3:5, 16; 17:6).

The book of Leviticus is set in the wilderness, after the people of Israel have left Egypt and before they enter Canaan. In that setting, bringing all animals slaughtered for food to the tabernacle was theoretically possible. But what about when Israel was settled in its land and had become a nation? Bringing an animal to the temple in Jerusalem every time you wanted to eat meat would be impossible in a time without automobiles. Even with a car it would still be way inconvenient.

Another law deals with precisely this issue. It commands sacrificing only at "the place that Yahweh will choose," i.e., the temple in Jerusalem (Deut. 12:13–14). It agrees with the prohibition against eating blood (12:16, 23–27). However, it also makes allowance for eating meat in the event that the temple is too far away. It does this by drawing a distinction between sacred or ritual slaughter and secular slaughter simply to provide meat, and it uses the analogy of wild game. You don't have to sacrifice part of an animal that has been killed in hunting, so domestic animals that are consumed just for food don't have to be sacrificed either (12:15, 22). The idea here may be that God is like a feudal lord who has to be compensated for any animals that are killed on his property, which includes Israel and its domestic animals but not wild ones. However, the real motive behind the distinguishing of secular and sacred slaughter in Deuteronomy is its emphasis on the doctrine of "centralization," the notion that there is only one place where God can properly be worshipped, namely the Temple in Jerusalem. All other shrines to Yahweh are invalid and forbidden.

This raises the question of the relationship between Leviticus 17 and Deuteronomy 12. They are obviously contradictory. Leviticus says that if you want to eat meat you have to take your domestic animal to the tabernacle to make a sacrifice; Deuteronomy says that you may slaughter animals for meat without going to sacrifice. Scholars struggle to explain this contradiction. Some argue that it is a matter of terminology and that if you understand the different verbal nuances (*slaughter* versus *sacrifice*) the contradiction disappears. Others propose that one of the laws is older than the other and that the practice of sacrifice changed at different periods. Still others conclude that the two laws simply reflect different perspectives on sacrifice from different groups in ancient Israel. Whatever the explanation for their difference, it is clear that both Leviticus and Deuteronomy regard sacrifice as central to their understanding of religion and the worship of God.

Law

The disagreement between Leviticus and Deuteronomy over sacrifice and the eating of meat raises the question of how law was practiced in ancient Israel. We'll skip the lawyer jokes except to point out that practice doesn't always make perfect. It is worthwhile noting, though, that we shouldn't read our legal system into the Bible's. In the United States we have a constitution, written at the beginning of the country, that provides the structure for our government and the basis for interpretation about specific legal issues. We tend to think of the law in the Bible the same way. That is, we think of it—and in fairness, it is presented this way—as a "constitution" delivered to Moses on Mount Sinai that served as a guide to Israel's daily life. Like everything dealing with law, it's a lot more complicated than that.

First of all, the Hebrew word translated "law"—*torah*—actually means "instruction." The Bible's *Torah* functioned as a source for religious teaching rather than as a roadmap for Israelite society. We've already seen that the *Torah* in the first five books of the Hebrew Bible contains not just a single set of laws but several different collections, the "Holiness Code" in Leviticus 17–26 for one, the "Ten Commandments" (Exod. 20; Deut. 5) for another. In other words, the *Torah* is not a single constitution but a collection or compilation of several different law codes.

Scholars debate when the different codes were written. The *Torah* as we have it, though, was compiled toward the end of Israel's history rather than written at the beginning. So it could not have functioned as a constitution. The different codes apparently emerged from different groups in Israel at different times in its history. They also had different purposes. Some, such as the Ten Commandments, may have represented principles distilled from previous decisions. Collections like this of absolute or "apodictic" law with direct commands ("Thou shalt not . . .") are rare in both the Bible and the ancient Near East. Much more common are collections of case or "casuistic" law. These "if . . . then" laws dealing with specific cases may have been written down as precedents or memory aids for future use.

Law codes could also serve as propaganda documents promoting the agenda or perspective of a particular group or individual. Consider the famous Code of Hammurapi from the Babylonian king of that name in the eighteenth century BCE. Its form suggests that it was not a document for courts or judges to consult on a routine basis. It is written on a nine-foot-high monolith or "stele" of black basalt with a relief at the top depicting Hammurapi receiving the "tablets of destiny" from the sun god, Shamash, who was also the god of justice. Its function seems to have been to promote the idea that Hammurapi was a divinely appointed ruler and a just king.

The point is that Moses was not Thomas Jefferson, nor was the law in the Hebrew Bible a constitution that was consulted in Israel's courts on a daily basis. For one thing, the Hebrew Bible originated long before the invention of the printing press; even if all of the Hebrew Bible law had been written at the time, not every city would have had a copy. Also, none of the collections is comprehensive. How could they be? It would be impossible to cover every single contingency in every conceivable case that might come before a court. There is overlap between some of the codes in the kinds of cases considered and also in their decisions. The Code of Hammurapi contains laws that are similar to some in the Bible even though it predates Moses by five hundred years. So there may have been a legal tradition that for the most part was passed on orally between countries and generations in the ancient Near East, of which Israel was a part.

How, then, did this legal system function? We don't know all the details. But we have hints in biblical and Near Eastern literature. Deuteronomy, for instance, speaks a lot about city elders as well as judges, indicating that legal decisions were local affairs in urban centers, though again perhaps based on oral traditions or codes. Deuteronomy also locates the courtroom in the city gate, and this is where the legal action in the book of Ruth takes place (Ruth 4:1–2). City gates were passageways with rooms and towers above them on either side of the path; benches lined the walls of those rooms. So when the prophet Amos condemns the treatment of the poor "in the gate" and calls for establishing justice there (Amos 5:12–15), he is critiquing Israel's court system.

There are other fascinating glimpses within the Bible of Israel's legal system at work, and we'd love to know more about it. There are cases like Solomon's famous judgment to cut a baby in half in order to discern its true mother (1 Kings 3:16–28), where the king renders a decision and seems to serve as the "supreme court." There are others, though, where the king seems subject to law or tradition and dependent on the court's decision. Thus, in 1 Kings 21, King Ahab wants land that he cannot have because it is part of a family's ancestral holdings. Queen Jezebel conspires with the elders and nobles of the landowner's city to bring him up on false charges aired by two witnesses so that he'll be executed and she can take over his land. From stories like these we are able to form a partial picture of how law functioned in ancient Israel, but there are still plenty of pieces missing.

Covenant

A covenant is basically a treaty. Just like today, treaties were an important part of international relations in the ancient Near East. As a result, a number of treaty documents have been preserved. There were two kinds of treaties: those between two equal kings or states, called parity treaties, and those between a superior and an inferior, called suzerainty or vassal treaties. Leviticus and Deuteronomy both contain treaty elements. Deuteronomy was even built at one stage of its development on the form of a vassal treaty between Yahweh and Israel. There are six structural elements of vassal treaties: (1) preamble identifying the treaty parties (Deut. 4:44–49); (2) historical prologue recounting the parties' past relationship (chs. 5–11); (3) stipulations undertaken by each of the parties (12:1–26:15); (4) instructions for deposition and periodic reading of treaty documents (10:1–5; 31:9–13, 24–26); (5) witnesses to the treaty (4:26; 30:19; 31:28) and loyalty oaths of the parties (26:16–19; 29:10–29); and (6) blessings and curses for obedience or disobedience of the treaty stipulations (28:1–68).

Of these elements, the curses and blessings in Deuteronomy 28 are particularly important. First, Leviticus 26 has a similar set of curses and blessings. Second, the list in Deuteronomy 28 is the longest and most detailed such list of all treaty documents from the ancient Near East. Third, several of the curses in it bear striking similarity to seventh-century Assyrian treaties, indicating that this was the origin of the form behind Deuteronomy. Fourth, and most important for our present purposes, treaty curses provide background for understanding several other texts and stories in the Hebrew Bible.

To begin with, there is the language of love and hate in treaties. Those who are loyal to their overlord and keep their obligations according to the treaty are said to "love" the suzerain—the controlling ruler or nation. Those who disobey are called the "enemies" of the suzerain and are said to "hate" him. When Deuteronomy talks about loving God with all one's heart, soul, and might (Deut. 6:5), it is really talking about keeping the commandments of the law, which are the stipulations in the treaty. So immediately following the command to love God come the mandates to "keep these words that I am commanding you today" and to teach them to children (Deut. 6:6–9).

The ceremony of making a treaty revolved to a large extent around the curses. In such ceremonies, which have been recorded in documents outside of the Bible, the parties used animals to take upon themselves the curses they would bear if they should ever break the treaty. They cut animals in pieces as a way of saying, "May I (or my animals) be cut in pieces if I should ever break this treaty." It's the same principle as when you say, "I'll be damned if I'm going to let him get away with that." Cutting animals may seem strange, but it's less radical than eternal damnation.

This is exactly the scene in Genesis 15 where Abraham cuts several animals in half and lays the halves against each other for symbols of God to pass between. Here God is making a promise to Abraham and is solemnizing it by symbolically taking up the curses for not fulfilling the promise. In other stories in the Bible, cut up pieces of an animal or even of a human are used to summon the tribes of Israel to war by reminding them of their treaty obligation to rally in support of a treaty partner (Judg. 19:29; 1 Sam. 11:7). The tribes are being reminded: "You signed on the dotted line, now it's time to pony up. And here's what you'll get if you don't."

Speaking of just desserts, treaty curses provide a rich source for the threats that the prophets level against Israel for disobeying Yahweh. These involve pretty much every kind of disaster you can think of: drought, famine, disease, invasion, earthquake. You name it. Amos and Micah and others get very creative, and the treaties are their source. What they are saying, though, boils down to this: "Because you have broken the treaty with God by disobeying the laws in the covenant God made with you, you have brought these curses upon you. Your only hope is to change your ways immediately and seek God's forgiveness."

These examples show that it's hard to overstate the importance of treaties as cultural background to the Hebrew Bible.

Second Helping

Eating meat at sacrifices was so common in the ancient world that we encounter it again in the New Testament, in one of the most interesting books in the Bible for the study of cultural background: 1 Corinthians. This book is a letter from Paul to the Christians in the city of Corinth. Despite its name, it was not the first letter Paul wrote to them. He refers to an earlier letter in 1 Corinthians 5:9, which is lost to us (unless it is incorporated within the First and Second Corinthians that we have). He also mentions a letter they wrote to him. We don't have that one either, but we can guess at its contents because he refers to it quite a bit and even quotes from it, if the NRSV translation is correct; we can't be sure because ancient Greek had no quotation marks.

The Corinthians had a lot of questions about their new religion. Not deep theological questions, but questions about practicalities relating to their daily lives. The questions point to what was happening on a broader scale. Christianity was expanding beyond its roots in Judaism and Palestine into the larger world. How would it work in other cultures? What accommodations would it have to make? Corinth was an interesting cultural mix. It was a Greek city that had been destroyed by the Romans in 146 BCE and then rebuilt in 44 BCE. It was rebuilt by the Romans as a model Roman city and the center of imperial Roman culture in Greece. How Christianity adapted to Corinth might determine how it would do in Rome and the whole

Roman Empire. So there was a lot at stake in how Paul answered the Corinthians' questions.

One of the topics in the exchange between Paul and the Corinthians was idolatry. Christianity was incompatible with the worship of idols, of course. But what constituted idol worship? Was it worship to eat some of the meat of a sacrifice to a pagan god, which was sold in markets? The letter writers in Corinth didn't think so. And Paul agreed. Quoting them he wrote, "No idol in the world really exists," and, "There is no God but one" (1 Cor. 8:3). The viewpoint of these people, who are called the "strong," was that eating food offered to idols didn't mean anything because there was no ultimate reality behind the statues.

But Paul has another concern, namely people he calls the "weak," those who have scruples about food offered to idols and would violate their consciences by eating it. His statement that they "have become so accustomed to idols until now, they still think of the food they eat as offered to idols" (8:7) indicates that at least some of the "weak" were Gentiles who had converted from polytheism. There may also have been a class difference behind the two groups. For poor people, public banquets were the only opportunities they had to eat meat, while those who were better off could buy meat whenever they wanted. In either case, the cultural background to this text suggests that the growing Christian movement struggled with some serious social distinctions just as churches today struggle with differences of race and class among their members.

Hair and Prayer

The cultural background of 1 Corinthians is especially important for one of the most curious passages in the New Testament: 1 Corinthians 11:3–16. Here Paul goes into a long diatribe about hair styles, veils, and gender dynamics. On the strength of this passage, women were required to wear some kind of head covering in church for many centuries. In the 1960s and '70s this passage was used by some to condemn men having long hair.

Unfortunately, no one really knows what's going on here, and NT scholars hotly debate this passage's meaning. Some of them think Paul is talking about head coverings (women should wear them, men shouldn't—vv. 4–5); others think he's interested in hair styles (men should have short hair, women long hair—vv. 14–15). At one point, Paul goes on a tangent expounding on Genesis to argue for a hierarchy in the church of God-Christ-man-woman (vv. 8–10), concluding that women need "a symbol of authority . . . because of the angels," whatever that means. The whole thing seems a bit petulant, especially when Paul ends by admitting that it is just a matter of custom (11:16). That's why we personally subscribe to George Carlin's first rule for starting a religion: no hats.

Actually, it is Paul's admission that he's talking about a custom that makes this text interesting. Since Paul clearly is discussing a custom, you can't make too much of the hierarchy he presents, as has often been done in past interpretation. When you think about it, the significance of cultural background for the passage is actually liberating. It shows that Paul is dealing here with a matter of custom and that this text should not be used, as it often has been, to subordinate women to men. Even more pointedly, his mention of a woman praying or prophesying (v. 5) clearly refers to a public deed and indicates women's active involvement in worship settings of the early church.

5 The Race Card

Ethnicity

Define *American*.

"Someone from America."

OK, what's *America*? The United States? What about South and Central America? And Canada? And does someone have to be born in one of these places to qualify? What about immigrants; are they Americans? What's an *Italian American* or an *Irish American* or an *African American*?

Consider a couple of friends of ours. One proudly refers to himself as Portuguese, even though he was born in the United States, has never been to Portugal, and knows only a few phrases of the language. The other was born in Mexico and grew up speaking Spanish. She immigrated as a teenager to the United States and speaks English with a distinct accent. However, she is quite firm that she is an American and a U.S. citizen, not a Mexican.

One of our colleagues, a fellow Bible scholar, is Jewish. He was born in Argentina, then emigrated with his family to Israel. He came to school in the United States and now lives in Canada. He calls himself a Jewish, Latino, Israeli, Canadian American. A Tiger Woods–like Bible scholar, if you will, only without the baggage.

Maybe *American* is, as they say, like porn: easier to recognize than it is to define.

In this chapter we're going to take on the issue of race, ethnicity, and national identity in the Bible. We'll take a stab at describing *Israelite*, which turns out to be as slippery as *American*. Our main concern, though, is showing the role that ethnicity plays in the Bible's narratives.

Our starting point is the books of Deuteronomy and Joshua. Deuteronomy articulates the concept of the chosen people and then Joshua fleshes it out in its account of Israel's conquest of Canaan and displacement of its inhabitants. We'll move on to later books in the Hebrew Bible that debate whether God exclusively favors Israel, with Ezra and Nehemiah on one side of the debate and Ruth and Jonah on the other. Finally we'll discuss the significance of ethnic identity in the early church in passages from the book of Acts and Paul's letters.

WHO'S AN ISRAELITE?

The Bible is full of "–ites." Certain texts in the Bible have lists of them, like Genesis 15:18–21, where God tells Abram, "To your descendants I give this land, from the river of Egypt to the great river, the river Euphrates, the land of the Kenites, the Kenizzites, the Kadmonites, the Hittites, the Perizzites, the Rephaim, the Amorites, the Canaanites, the Girgashites, and the Jebusites." Who were all these people? What were the differences among them? The truth is we don't know much about them. The distinctions, whatever they might have been, aren't very clear to us now.

And yet racial and ethnic identities have theological significance in the Bible. The Bible calls the Israelites God's chosen people, so maybe we can at least define who they were. Again, this turns out to be easier said than done. First of all, contrary to common opinion, Israelites, Hebrews, and Jews were not all the same thing. Sometimes the terms overlap, but they can also be used to distinguish different categories of people. *Israelite* was a term for national origin. In Hebrew, it's the same as the modern term *Israeli*, though without the same sense of nationhood that exists in the modern world. The two words are identical in Hebrew; it's only in English that *Israelite* refers to an ancient citizen of Israel, while *Israeli* means a citizen of the modern country. In the Bible, *Israelite* is also an ethnic designation: all Israelites are thought of as descendants of a single ancestor, Israel or Jacob, and then his grandfather, Abraham. But this was clearly a secondary development. The Bible stories themselves admit that not all Israelites were descended from Jacob.

Hebrew is the name of a language, of course. But when used for people it was apparently a social designation referring to people who lived on the fringes of settled society as mercenaries and raiders. In the Bible, when the term occurs, it is usually in the mouths of non-Israelites talking about Israelites. If Israelites use it in reference to themselves, it is in conversation with foreigners.[1] Bottom line: the name *Hebrews* could refer to Israelites, but was not their preferred term for themselves, maybe because it implied a lower social status.

Jews originated from *Judeans* but became a term that could denote both religious and ethnic affiliation. The two meanings overlap to a large extent. People who are Jews by religion are almost always ethnic Jews. However, Judaism as a religion is not synonymous with the religion of ancient Israel. Judaism has its roots in the Hebrew Bible, but it is really a later development—an extension of the religion of ancient Israel. Judaism evolved into the religion it is today starting at about the same time as Christianity. They were and are contemporary and competing interpretations of the traditions found in the Hebrew Bible.

Like America, ancient Israel was a melting pot, with people of different ethnic origins. Abraham came from Ur of the Chaldeans (Gen. 11:31), which might make him Mesopotamian (i.e., from ancient Iraq). Alternatively, he may have been one of the people that the Mesopotamians called Amorites, meaning "Westerners." There were a lot of Amorites in southern Mesopotamia in the first half of the second millennium (2000–1500) BCE when the Abraham stories are set. Jacob is called "a wandering Aramean" (Deut. 26:5), another term for "Syrian." The births of all of Jacob's children except Benjamin took place in Aram/Syria according to Genesis 29–30, and their mothers were Arameans. This would make the tribes of Israel Aramean as well. To complicate matters further, Exodus 12:38 says that the people who came out of Egypt were a "mixed crowd," i.e., of different racial, ethnic, and national origins. Maybe there were some Egyptians mixed in. Perhaps also there were people of other origins and ethnicities who had been enslaved with the Israelites in Egypt

---

[1] See Sarah Mandell, "Hebrew, Hebrews," in *Eerdmans Dictionary of the Bible*, ed. David Noel Freedman (Grand Rapids, MI: Eerdmans, 2000), 567–68.

and took advantage of the opportunity to escape with them. It was like one big Ellis Island.

One of the reasons for so many different ethnic origins is literary. The stories about Abraham, Jacob, and the Exodus are competing "foundation traditions." They give different accounts of Israel's national origins or foundation. The fact is, from a strictly historical perspective we don't know exactly where the people of Israel came from. Maybe there were different foundation traditions because people of different ethnic groups came to constitute Israel, and each group had its own origin tradition. Some groups traced their heritage back to Abraham, others back to Jacob, and still others back to the Exodus generation. The once-independent foundation stories were subsequently combined into a sequence. That's all pretty speculative. But how else can you explain the stories of different origins?

There's even a fourth foundation story of sorts. The book of Joshua continues the Exodus story by telling about the Israelites' conquest of Canaan. It includes some stories about groups of Canaanite people being "absorbed" into Israel. The best-known examples are Rahab and her family (Josh. 2; 6) and the Gibeonites (Josh. 9). What makes these stories especially interesting is that archaeology tends to confirm the origins of Israel within the land of Canaan. The best and most recent archaeology indicates that when it comes to the artifacts they left behind, the people who became known as Israel had their beginnings in a village culture in the highlands of Canaan. They may have been joined by other population groups from elsewhere, which would explain the other foundation traditions. But basically, the Israelites were originally Canaanites.

THE CHOSEN PEOPLE

Having Canaanites as another ingredient to the melting pot that was ancient Israel really changes the flavor of the stew. That's because of what the books of Deuteronomy and Joshua say you're supposed to do to the Canaanites. You're supposed to wipe them out. In the words of Deuteronomy 7:2, "You must utterly destroy them . . . show them no mercy." This includes men, women, children, and even animals, as detailed in the story of the fall of Jericho (Josh. 6:21). Everything else was burned, except for the valuable metals, which were deposited into the treasury of the tabernacle (Josh. 6:19).

Another tradition, in Genesis 9, doesn't go quite as far. It justifies the enslavement of the Canaanites rather than their annihilation. The reason? Try this on for size. After the flood, Noah planted a vineyard. With the grapes he made wine, got drunk, and lay around naked in his tent. His son Ham saw him naked. When Noah woke up and found out he cursed Ham's son, Canaan, and his offspring with slavery. Quite a stretch, eh? It's pretty obvious that this text is trying to legitimate oppression of the Canaanites and taking over their land. What's even weirder is how this text has been interpreted in our own history to justify slavery and racial segregation. Just do an online search for "curse of Ham" sometime.

So where did all of this animosity toward Canaanites come from? In part, it was from the general ideology in the ancient Near East about the relationship of nations and gods. The notion was that each god had its own people or nation; each people had its own god. Deuteronomy 32:8–9 sums up the idea nicely:

> When the Most High apportioned the nations, when he divided humankind
> He fixed the boundaries of the peoples according to the number of the gods;
> the LORD's own portion was his people, Jacob his allotted share.

In other words, way back when at some point the gods got together to divide up the nations and peoples of the world, Yahweh got Israel and vice versa. Monotheism had obviously not developed yet. You were supposed to worship the god on whose land you lived. Biblical writers looking back and trying to explain Israel's origins understood the land of Canaan as belonging to Yahweh, who was giving it to Israel. That meant that all the people and animals in the land that were not Israelites and did not worship Yahweh were trespassing and had to be destroyed. They were to be slaughtered or "devoted" as a sacrifice to Yahweh. It was a kind of "holy war." And it wasn't unique to Israel. We have references to the same practice, even the same word for "devotion," in inscriptions outside of the Bible. This background suggests that the "Canaanites" in Deuteronomy and Joshua may be a kind of code for nonworshippers of Yahweh. Of course, whatever the context and whether it was for ethnic or religious reasons, this kind of genocide or "ethnic cleansing" is still morally reprehensible. So the fact that the Bible commands it is deeply disturbing.

The good news is it probably never happened. The wholesale slaughter of people described in the book of Joshua was probably more posturing and propaganda for theological reasons, long after the fact, than the recording of historical events. [We explored this matter of history in chapter 3.] But the uncertainty and probable diversity of Israel's origins and the different foundation traditions already suggest that the story of the conquest of Canaan was a later, oversimplified attempt to explain how Israel came to be.

Also, if read carefully, there's a sense in which the Bible's conquest stories actually undermine the element of genocide. The utter destruction of the native population never works. There are always survivors. And some of these survivors are pretty important in the long run. We've already mentioned Rahab. A prostitute in Jericho, she sheltered the spies that Joshua sent ahead in exchange for her life and the lives of her family when the city fell. Without her, the Israelites might not have been able to conquer Jericho, or it would not have gone so smoothly. Even more important, Rahab and her family were absorbed into Israel and became a part of it, and she became one of the ancestors of the likes of David and Jesus (Matt. 1:5).

Beyond the conquest story in Joshua, the book of Judges begins by listing groups of Canaanites that the Israelites did not or could not annihilate or drive out and who were presumably eventually absorbed into Israel. Later on, during the reign of David there are multiple references to people of various ethnicities who are part of Israel, including Hittites (2 Sam. 11), Cushites (2 Sam. 18:21–32), and even Philistines (2 Sam. 15:18–22).

In fact, King David himself, the great founder of Israel as a nation, was not pure Israelite, as if there were such a thing. Even before Rahab there was Tamar, a Canaanite woman who saved the tribe of Judah from extinction according to Genesis 38. And a third foreign woman listed in David's genealogy is Ruth, who came from the country of Moab on the other side of the Dead Sea from Israel. Without foreigners there would have been no David and no Israel either, for that matter.

UNIVERSALISM

The book of Ruth depicts its namesake not only as David's great-great-grandmother (Ruth 4:21–22) but also as a model of the virtues of love and loyalty. She promises her mother-in-law, Naomi,

> Where you go, I will go;
>> where you lodge, I will lodge;
> your people shall be my people,
>> and your God my God. (1:16)

And she keeps her word, leaving her homeland in Moab and returning with Naomi to Judah. She supports the two of them by gleaning in the fields. She adopts Naomi's people and her religion despite what the book of Deuteronomy has to say about Moabites: "No Ammonite or Moabite shall be admitted to the assembly of the Lord. Even to the tenth generation, none of their descendants shall be admitted to the assembly of the Lord" (Deut. 23:3). But Ruth characterizes exactly the sort of person you would want as part of your people or "assembly." In other words, the story of Ruth effectively counters Deuteronomy on this point.

It may be that Ruth was written as part of an ongoing debate about non-Israelites or non-Jews in the period following the Babylonian exile. On one side of the debate stood Ezra and Nehemiah. They were leading the effort to rebuild the temple and reinstitute worship there following the return from exile. They interpreted the laws in Deuteronomy about foreigners as referring to the people remaining in the land who had not gone into exile. They both commanded the returnees who had married "native" women to divorce them and their children (Ezra 10; Neh. 13:23–27). The reason for such a harsh attitude was the need they felt to consolidate the returnees in the face of opposition and resentment from the local leaders.

On the other side were Ruth and Jonah, among other biblical books. They advocated a theological viewpoint known as "Universalism"—the idea that God cares for everyone, not just those of a certain nation or race. The book of Jonah, as we have seen (chapter 1), uses satire to make fun of an attitude of prejudice embodied in the character of the ridiculous prophet Jonah. The book portrays God as being concerned about all of creation—even the hated Assyrians in Nineveh and their animals too. Ruth's main character is a Moabite woman who embodies the virtues held in esteem by Israelites and who was in the direct line of one of Israel's greatest heroes, King David. It cannot be proven that Jonah and Ruth were written specifically to counter Ezra and Nehemiah. But the attitude of Universalism represented in them certainly contrasts with the narrow measures put forward by Ezra and Nehemiah.

To sum up, ancient Israel was ethnically a melting pot of different backgrounds, but its basic constituency was Canaanite. The texts in Deuteronomy and Joshua that mandate annihilation or enslavement of people of other ethnicities (specifically Canaanites) were written to emphasize the importance of worshipping Yahweh alone. Ezra and Nehemiah interpreted Deuteronomy literally because of the need for unity of purpose in their work to rebuild Jerusalem and the Temple. Other books like Ruth and Jonah stress God's concern for people of all ethnicities and may have been written to counter Deuteronomy and the interpretation of it in Ezra-Nehemiah.

Jews and Gentiles: Defining Christianity

Jesus was a Jew. All of Jesus' earliest followers were Jews. Thus, at its beginning, Christianity was a Jewish sect. Its adherents were Jews who believed that Jesus of Nazareth was the Jewish Messiah. So when Christianity began to spread among non-Jews, i.e., "Gentiles," there were a lot of questions, and some growing pains.

Two books in the New Testament describe this process, but in very different ways. One of them is Paul's letter to the Galatians, which is one of the first books of the New Testament to have been written. Paul's letters usually begin with a section of encouragement and thanksgiving for his readers. Not so Galatians. Instead, after the customary greetings, he immediately begins to scold them (Gal. 1:6–9), and with very harsh language. He accuses them of turning to a different gospel (1:6), or rather following those who pervert the gospel (1:7). Then he twice pronounces damnation on those who teach this different gospel (1:8–9).

What had Paul so upset? Further reading in the letter shows that he was contending against the teachings of a group called "Judaizers," after the word Paul uses to describe the action of his opponents in 2:14. These people apparently taught that Gentiles who converted to Christianity had to follow the law in the Hebrew Bible, especially the rite of circumcision. Paul was adamantly opposed to this teaching and argued that the law, as important as it had been, was not a requirement for Gentile followers of Jesus.

The Judaizers may have attacked Paul personally, or at least his credentials. They may also have had some affiliation with Jerusalem and some of the church leaders there, especially Peter. This is indicated by Paul's discussion of his conversion and early ministry in the first two chapters of Galatians. He makes the point that he was converted and given his gospel through a personal revelation of Jesus.

> For I did not receive it from a human source, nor was I taught it, but I received it through a revelation of Jesus Christ. (Gal. 1:12)

> But when God, who had set me apart before I was born and called me through his grace, was pleased to reveal his Son to me, so that I might proclaim him among the Gentiles, I did not confer with any human being. (Gal. 1:15–16)

Paul goes on to state that he did not go to Jerusalem or Damascus immediately after his conversion but went away into Arabia (1:17), visiting Jerusalem only three years later—and seeing only Peter on that occasion (1:18–19). Fourteen years after that, he says, he went to Jerusalem to meet with the leaders there and was welcomed by them. They endorsed his mission to Gentiles without compelling him to teach circumcision (2:1–9). The only thing they asked him to do was to "remember the poor"—probably a request that he take up a collection for the Christians in Jerusalem, who had recently experienced famine (1 Cor. 16:1–4; 2 Cor. 8–9). But then later on when Peter (= Cephas) came to visit Paul in Antioch, Paul accused him of acting hypocritically because he refused to eat with the Gentile Christians out of fear of the "circumcision faction" affiliated with James (Gal. 2:11–12).

These verses hint at what may have been a very bitter rift between Paul and the church leaders in Jerusalem, including Peter and James. And the cause of the rift was disagreement over matters related to race and ethnicity.

The version of these events in the book of Acts (ch. 9) is very different. Acts and Galatians both agree that Paul (= Saul) persecuted Christians before he became one himself. But other than that, they have little in common. Acts tells about Paul seeing a light and hearing Jesus' voice from heaven as he approached Damascus (Acts 9:3–7). Blinded by the light (quick, find the oldies station), he was led into the city, where a Christian man named Ananias visited him and healed his blindness (9:8–19). He stayed in Damascus and began preaching Christianity until a plot on his life forced him to flee (9:19–25).

None of this is in Paul's own version in Galatians. And there is a clear contradiction in Paul's statement that he immediately left for Arabia and only later returned to Damascus (Gal. 1:17). Acts' further account that Paul went from Damascus to Jerusalem, where he was eventually accepted because of Barnabas's charity (Acts 9:26–30), also contradicts Paul's claim that he did not go to Jerusalem until three years later and then saw no other apostle except James (Gal. 1:18–19).

In Acts, the event that brings the Gentile issue to the attention of the Jerusalem leadership is the conversion of the Roman centurion Cornelius, and the one who teaches him is Peter, not Paul (Acts 10). Cornelius was not the first Gentile to become a Christian according to Acts. That distinction belonged to a black man: the Ethiopian eunuch (Acts 8:26–39). But it was Cornelius's case that drew attention. At least that's the way the book of Acts has it. This may, however, reflect one of the particular interests of the author of Acts—namely, the wish to show that Christianity was not opposed to the Roman Empire. Hence, the "test case" for the conversion of Gentiles is a Roman military officer.

In any case, as Acts describes it, Cornelius's conversion raises the question of whether Gentiles can be accepted "as is" into Christianity or whether they need first to be circumcised and follow Jewish law. In Acts, this matter comes before the church leaders in Jerusalem, and it represents a watershed moment for the book of Acts and the newborn church. The "council" of leaders in Acts 15 determines that God, by bestowing the Holy Spirit on Gentile believers, has already shown that Gentiles are to be accepted as they are without any requirements to follow Jewish practice. They do ask, though, that the Gentiles abstain "from things polluted by idols, and from fornication and from whatever has been strangled and from blood" (Acts 15:20) or "from what has been sacrificed to idols and from blood and from what is strangled and from fornication" (15:29). It's not certain exactly what was meant by these prohibitions, but they appear to be things about which Jews would be especially sensitive or that they thought were universally applicable to Gentiles as well as Jews.

In Galatians 2:1–10, Paul also alludes to the Jerusalem Council, but again there are significant differences. He does not mention Cornelius, or Peter's role in converting him. Rather, he says that this gathering acknowledged that he, Paul, "had been entrusted with the gospel for the uncircumcised, just as Peter had been entrusted with the gospel for the circumcised" (2:7). That is, in Paul's version, Peter is not associated with the mission to the Gentiles at all. Nor does he mention the letter of the Jerusalem leaders with the list of things Gentiles should avoid. Their only stipulation, according to Paul, was remembering the poor.

Despite their differences about details, Acts and Galatians are in agreement that the first real internal controversy faced by the early church was a racial one. What was to be done with Gentiles who converted to what was originally a Jewish movement? The differences between the accounts in the two books suggest that the division over this question was deeply rooted. There was also a divide over leadership, with Peter and Paul as the two main contenders. In a sense, perhaps there were two (at least) Christianities or major factions of Christianity. This is potentially a consolation to modern Christians faced with the divisions among Orthodox, Catholic, and Protestant, not to mention the plethora of denominations within the Protestant tradition.

The differences between Acts and Galatians also reveal the variant interests of their authors. Paul defends himself and his ministry in Galatians. He wants to show that his gospel came directly from Jesus and not from any human source, so he discounts any contact with Jerusalem. The author of Acts, in contrast, emphasizes both the unity of the early church and the central role played by Jerusalem, at least at the beginning. So Acts attributes a larger role to the

Jerusalem leadership than does Paul and also downplays or ignores the split between Paul and Peter.

The role played by race and ethnicity in different parts of the Bible attests to the struggle of human beings to balance identification with one's own people (family, clan, tribe, etc.) with openness to others and an appreciation of the richness brought by diversity of perspective and tradition.

Is That What That Really Means?

chapter 6

Eewwphemisms

Pop quiz: What do the songs *Puff the Magic Dragon* and *Lucy in the Sky with Diamonds* have in common? If you said, "Illicit drug use," you're right, at least according to some popular interpretations.

The same thing is true about the Bible—not that the Bible has songs or stories about drug use, but it does have stories and expressions that are about something other than what they appear to be. These don't have to do with drugs or rock and roll, but they do concern other things that are generally considered most uncharacteristic of the Bible, namely sex and scatology (a fancy term for stuff having to do with urination and defecation). In fact, some people might consider it blasphemous even to speak about such topics in the same breath or context as the Bible. We think, though, that this is a mark of the Bible's richness. It's a collection of literature that deals with life in all of its dimensions, the sublime and spiritual, as well as the common and down-to-earth.[1]

One reason people don't recognize how much the Bible discusses sex and bodily functions is that it often does so in creative literary ways by the use of euphemisms and double entendres. A euphemism is a more polite or genteel way of referring to a delicate subject. We use euphemisms a lot. Like when we say that someone "passed away" in order to avoid speaking of death. For sex, we talk

---

[1] We've written a whole book evaluating these kinds of interpretations of the Bible. See John Kaltner, Steven L. McKenzie, and Joel Kilpatrick, *The Uncensored Bible: The Bawdy and Naughty Bits of the Good Book* (San Francisco: HarperOne, 2008).

about "sleeping together," or in more recent parlance, "hooking up." When it comes to bodily functions, our personal euphemism of choice (probably because we're guys) is "going to see a man about a horse." *Double entendre* is French for "double meaning." A double entendre is like a euphemism but more subtle. Rather than actually meaning something else, a double entendre, as the name implies, has a more obvious "surface" meaning and another, "deeper," and usually bawdy implication. If you're an aficionado of *The Office*, with its running "that's what she said" gag, or you've ever seen a James Bond flick with character names like Pussy Galore, you're familiar with lewd double entendres.

The Bible makes generous use of both euphemisms and double entendres in some of its stories. In this chapter, we're going to explore some of the Bible's more colorful stories and expose the real meanings behind their expressions and images. We actually have a serious and legitimate reason for doing this. It isn't to exercise our puerile senses of humor. Well, OK, not for that alone. Showing what is really going on in these stories is a way of demonstrating the importance of reading Bible narratives in their full literary contexts and, at the same time, of paying close attention to the language of those narratives. Our beginning point is the book of Judges, which contains a collection of some of the most unusual stories in the Bible.

Lefty versus Fatty

The first real judge in the book is named Ehud. His story is in Judges 3. Technically, there is one judge earlier than Ehud whose name is Othniel. But there aren't many details in the Othniel story (Judg. 3:7–11), and most scholars think that he serves simply to provide a model of the circular pattern subscribed to by the stories of the judges (sin—foreign oppression—repentance—deliverance by a judge—tranquility—sin—etc.).

Ehud was left-handed. However, the Hebrew expression literally refers to someone whose right hand was bound or restricted. This may mean that Ehud was specially trained to use his left hand in order to gain an advantage in hand-to-hand combat. Ehud's opponent, who was oppressing Israel, was the king of Moab (the country on the other side of the Dead Sea from Israel). His name was Eglon. "Eglon" means "calf," and he is described as being very fat (3:17). This not-so-subtle depiction of Eglon as a fatted calf might be double entendre, suggesting to the reader that Eglon will be slaughtered, as indeed he is, by Ehud. Here's where Ehud's left-handedness plays a role in the story. It accounts for how he is able to sneak a sword past Eglon's guards when he gets a private audience with the king by claiming he has a secret message for his ears only. The guards assume that Ehud is right-handed and search only his left side where a right-handed man would sheathe his sword. This also suggests an element of ridicule in the story, making fun of Moabites for being too stupid and gullible to search Ehud more thoroughly.

The story of Ehud's assassination of Eglon in Judges 3:20–25 makes use of several terms and expressions, especially architectural ones, that are rare or even unique in the Hebrew Bible. In some cases, the meanings are relatively clear from the context. In others, the exact meaning remains elusive. An example of the former is the word translated "dirt" (NRSV) in 3:22. It occurs only here. It is evident in the context that the word refers to the contents of Eglon's stomach or, more likely, his colon. "Dirt," therefore, is euphemistic, and a better rendering would probably be "feces" or the like. This is important to the story, because it explains why the guards assumed that Eglon was relieving himself (v. 24). The expression here rendered "relieving himself" literally means "covering his feet." It occurs one other place in the Hebrew Bible as part of a degrading picture of Saul when he is in pursuit of David (1 Sam. 24:3). In both passages the expression is transparently a euphemism for defecation derived from the practice of dropping one's garments on one's feet while assuming the required squatting posture. In the Judges story, Eglon's servants assume he's defecating because they smell the odor emitted from the contents of his colon. The "roof chamber" mentioned in 3:20–25 was probably actually a bathroom.

The unpleasant end of Eglon is narrated as a piece of scatological humor. It describes the circumstances of the king's death in great detail, relishing the frequent references to bodily functions. In this way, it demeans Israel's enemies, the Moabites and their king, not only by presenting them as stupid but also by associating them with human offal.

Deborah and Jael

The Ehud story is exceptional for its disgusting focus on toilet activities. Most double entendre is in the service of sexual innuendo. That is certainly the case in the story of Ehud's successor, Deborah (Judg. 4–5). Deborah (whose name means "bee") is the only female judge. The commander of the Israelite army whom she sends to war against the oppressing Canaanites is named Barak. His refusal to fight without her indicates that gender and sexual politics will play a leading role in this story.

Deborah informs Barak that his enemy will be killed by a woman, and so it happens—twice. Actually, the story is told twice—once in prose (ch. 4) and again in poetry (ch. 5). The poem is widely regarded as one of the oldest pieces of literature in the Bible, and the prose version creatively interprets it. The two versions differ in their respective details, most notably in the way Sisera is killed. The poem uses parallelism (saying the same thing in two different lines), which is the hallmark of Hebrew poetry. It tells how Jael takes some "blunt instrument" associated with tent dwelling—a tent peg or a mallet—and smashes Sisera's head with it so that he falls down dead (5:26–27). The prose story, in contrast, has Jael use a hammer to drive a tent peg through Sisera's skull and into the ground where she has coaxed him into lying (4:21).

Both versions are rife with double entendre and sexual innuendo. The scene in the prose story is a kind of seduction, especially considering what usually happens in the Bible when a man and a woman are alone together in a private setting. Jael goes out to meet Sisera and invites him into her tent. She slakes his thirst and literally lays him down to sleep. In killing him, Jael reverses sexual roles as she penetrates his body with the phallic-shaped tent peg. The language of the poem is full of double entendres. The verbs in verses 26–27 (sink, lie, fall) can all be used in sexual contexts, and the expression translated "at her feet" (NRSV) literally means "between her legs."

The sexual connotations are especially evident in the final scene of the poem (5:28–31) where Sisera's mother is seen worrying about her son's delay in returning home. She soothes herself with the thought that he and his men are enjoying the spoils of victory—especially the women captives: "a girl or two for every man" (5:30).

The Hebrew word translated "girl" is literally "womb." It's a euphemism for the female sexual organs. Sisera and his companions would not be interested in reproducing with the women captives, only in raping them. The irony is that Sisera's mother is right about what her son is doing. Sort of. He is engaged in a kind of rape or violation, but as the victim rather than the perpetrator. The poem and its prose counterpart artfully use euphemisms, double entendres, and sexual innuendo to drive home this irony.

Samson and Delilah

We can hardly discuss sexual politics and gender dynamics in Judges without taking a look at the story of Samson, even though it doesn't exhibit the same kinds of euphemisms and double entendres. It is, however, full of sexual tension—a classic story of the battle of the sexes. Samson is the rugged, brawny hero who repeatedly carries out deeds of superhuman strength: killing a lion with his bare hands (Judg. 14:6), setting fire to the Philistines' fields with torches tied to the tails of 150 pairs of foxes (15:4–5), slaying 1,000 Philistines with the fresh jawbone of a donkey (15:15), wrenching up the enormous wood and iron gates of the city of Gaza from their sockets and carrying them overnight some forty-plus miles to Hebron (16:3).

Obviously, Samson and the Philistines had a rivalry going on, and they were desperate to stop him. So they turned to a woman, Delilah. Samson had a weakness for women, especially Philistine women, as the stories in Judges 14–15 show. Delilah is commissioned to discover the secret of Samson's great strength. She goes about her task with utter honesty. She never lies to Samson, according to the story in Judges 16. She simply asks him where his strength lies and then tries out whatever he tells her—tying him with seven fresh bowstrings, then with new ropes, then weaving his hair with a loom. Each time, he breaks free easily. She never tells him that she loves him, but she accuses him of not loving her and of making fun of her by constantly lying to her.

Finally, when Samson can't stand her nagging and cajoling any longer, he tells her the truth (16:16–17). This, of course, brings his downfall. She lulls him to sleep upon her knees. Here there is just a hint of sexual activity. Or is the image maternal? Or both? She summons the barber to shave his head while he sleeps, and his strength disappears. He will regain just enough of it to kill himself along with 3,000 Philistines by collapsing the packed temple of their god, Dagon (16:23–30). Meanwhile, Delilah, having received her payment from the Philistines, disappears from the story and is never heard from again.

The sexual background of the Samson stories and especially the one involving Delilah leads readers to ponder their purpose and the reason for their inclusion in the book of Judges. The stories resemble the legends of figures like Paul Bunyan in their description of extraordinary deeds. They are certainly entertaining. But what is their theological value? Samson is not exactly a model of morality. He has liaisons with different women and kills a large number of Philistines, which seems to be heartily approved of in Judges. So do these stories simply celebrate the slaughter of Israel's enemies? Or are they intended as a cautionary tale about the purposelessness of violence and the ineffectiveness of brute strength? And what is the role of God in these stories? God ordains Samson's birth and inspires some of his most violent exploits (14:4, 6, 19; 15:14), but then departs from him mechanically when his hair is cut. It's not clear whether God responds to his cry for help at the end or not. There's no easy answer that we can see to these questions. Perhaps the most that can be said for certain is that the Samson tales with their penchant for outrageous sex and violence enhance the richness and diversity of the Bible's repertoire.

Jacob and Esau

Back to some more straightforward literary questions. Having seen in the Deborah story how perception of the sexual overtones can enrich the reading of a text, we can go back and apply our search for euphemisms and double entendres to the stories of Jacob and Esau in Genesis, where sexuality is crucial to the point and yet often overlooked. Two well-known cases will illustrate.

The first is the story of the birth of the twin brothers in Genesis 25:21–26. It describes a very odd set of circumstances. The two infants struggle in their mother's womb before Esau emerges all hairy and red. Jacob then follows grasping his brother's heel. The story is so rich in layers of meaning that it might be considered a triple or quadruple entendre. To begin with, the babies represent and embody the countries whose names they bear. Hence Rebekah is told that two nations or peoples are inside her (25:23). Jacob, also known as Israel, is the country of Israel. Esau is Edom (25:30). These names also account for their descriptions. Edom means "red," and the word for hair in Hebrew (*se'ar*) is a pun on Seir, another name for the country of Edom. "Jacob" sounds like the Hebrew word for "heel" (*'aqeb*). The verb form of the root has the sense of "supplant" or "replace" as well as the connotation of doing so by deceit. It thus explains Jacob's character in the following stories: Jacob supplants his brother as heir by craftily gaining first his birthright and then his blessing.

Another level of meaning in this story is sexual. The word *heel* occurs elsewhere in the Bible as a euphemism for the sexual organs. Specifically, in Jeremiah 13:22, the invasion of Israel (Judah) by a foreign army is depicted as the rape of a woman whose "skirts are lifted up" and whose "heels are violated." In Genesis 25, therefore, Jacob may be envisioned seizing Esau's sexual organs rather than his heel. This may seem to be an unnecessary interpretation and a stretch, until you consider that the larger context and point of the story is about heritage: the continuation of the line of Abraham and Isaac and who will be the rightful heir to the divine promise of the land and nation of Israel. Considering that the story is all about the patriarchal line, the notion that Jacob is born grasping Esau's procreative power is perfectly fitting.

The second Jacob story where this kind of double entendre and euphemism is at work is the one about Jacob's wrestling match in Genesis 32. After crossing the Jabbok River at night, Jacob is attacked by someone or something variously called a man, God, or an angel. The two struggle with each other until daybreak, when the opponent touches or strikes Jacob on the "hollow of the thigh," disabling him and causing him to limp the next morning. Jacob extracts a blessing from the being and his name is changed to Israel, ostensibly meaning "he wrestles with God." The story ends by explaining that this is the reason the Israelites do not eat the sinew or muscle on the "hollow of the thigh."

The word *thigh* is used several times in the Bible as a euphemism; Jacob's descendants in Exodus 1:5, for instance, are literally those who "come out of his thigh." There are also good reasons for taking the word *hollow* (*qaph*) as a reference to the groin or crotch. Jacob is disabled, therefore, because his opponent deals him a blow below the belt—which also explains why he limps the next morning. This would mean, further, that the sinew or muscle on the "hollow of the thigh" refers to the sexual organs, which are understandably considered off limits for purposes of consumption.

Again, this interpretation may seem inordinate upon first glance. However, in the larger context of the Jacob story and of Genesis it is entirely appropriate. In fact, it fits a lot better than the usual understanding of the sinew in question as the sciatic nerve. The issue, again, is the continuation of Jacob's line. Jacob has received notice that his brother Esau is coming to him with four hundred men. He fears that Esau still holds a grudge for Jacob's having supplanted him and that Esau will seek to do him harm. The wrestling episode provides reassurance to Jacob on two counts. First, the blow to the nether regions is a reminder that God is in charge of Jacob's reproductive powers and therefore of his family line and that Jacob need not fear anyone else. Second, the change of his name to Israel and the meaning associated with it assure Jacob that he and his descendants will prevail against Esau and all other opponents.

David and Michal

Back on the other side of Judges, Jacob's heirs are still fighting with the Philistines over territory, so Samson's career made no long-term difference. Israel has asked for and received a king to help it consolidate against external threats. King Saul soon proves unsatisfactory to God, who chooses David as a replacement. Saul loved David at first but is stirred to jealousy after his defeat of Goliath so that he now seeks a way to get rid of David.

An unusual opportunity presents itself when Saul learns that his own daughter, Michal, is in love with David (1 Sam. 18:20–21). Since David can't afford the bride price for a king's daughter, Saul proposes that he pay in Philistine hides—not complete hides, mind you, just foreskins. Saul figures that the Philistines will fight to the death to defend theirs and is hoping that David will die in the attempt to take them. Brilliant and twisted.

You might assume that the corroboration required by Saul of David is absolutely unique and unprecedented. Not so, as it turns out. What we have here is the practice of collecting war trophies. We're more familiar with it in the form of scalping. But it's a practice as old as the Egyptians. There are ancient Egyptian reliefs and inscriptions that both describe and depict piles of uncircumcised phalluses (as well as hands) being presented to the pharaoh as war trophies to show what slaughter his army had wrought against his enemies. The Egyptian word used for these uncircumcised members is the same as that used in the biblical text for foreskins.

This suggests that the trophies brought by David to Saul actually were entire phalluses rather than just foreskins. The story as it reads, though, presents a classic case of adding insult to injury. David "converts" the Philistines into Israelites by circumcising them after he has killed them. The story also reveals a different side of David in his relationship to Saul. He obviously has to risk his life in acquiring the trophies to bring to Saul. Why would he take such a risk? Careful reading indicates that it is not because he is in love with Michal. The text never says that. Rather, it speaks constantly about becoming the king's son-in-law. David risks his life not for love but for personal ambition. This is not a David who passively waits for God to create a place for him, but an ambitious figure who seeks power through self-advancement. Perhaps Saul was right to be afraid of this David.

Prophets and Kings

Fast-forwarding, David eventually replaces Saul as king of Israel. He is succeeded in turn by his own son, Solomon. After Solomon the kingdom divides between Israel in the north and Judah in the south. The main historical difference between the two kingdoms is that Judah is ruled throughout its history (until 586 BCE) by a single dynasty descended from David. Israel, by contrast, does not last as long (destroyed by Assyria in 722 BCE), and it goes through a series of dynasties or royal houses, each one typically overthrown and replaced in a coup d'etat led by the army. Think small South American country.

In the books of Samuel and Kings, these two different histories are explained etiologically through a scheme of prophecy and fulfillment. The endurance of the Davidic dynasty is prophesied by Nathan in 2 Samuel 7. In Kings, a series of prophets forecasts the downfall of each royal house in turn. Their oracles are nearly identical, indicating that they were actually composed by the book's author. The oracle against the house of Jeroboam, the first king of Israel following the division, is representative. It contains two parts, the first threatening the assassination of all the male members of Jeroboam's family, the second a curse of nonburial:

> Therefore, I will bring evil upon the house of Jeroboam. I will cut off from Jeroboam every male, both bond and free in Israel, and will consume the house of Jeroboam, just as one burns up dung until it is all gone. Anyone belonging to Jeroboam who dies in the city, the dogs shall eat; and anyone who dies in the open country, the birds of the air shall eat; for the LORD has spoken. (1 Kings 14:10–11)

The first part uses an expression for "male" that literally means "one who urinates on the wall." It is rendered very literally in the King James Version: "Him that pisseth against the wall." This expression highlights a key element of a usurper's strategy—to kill all the male heirs of his predecessor to avoid future retaliation from any of them. In grammatical terms, this expression is a synecdoche, a figure of speech in which a part is used to represent a whole. For example, a rancher's reference to "forty head" of cattle uses the head for the entire animal. In Kings, the body part used for males is the genitalia. To put it bluntly, it's calling them "dicks" or "pricks." This understanding is perfectly in line with the violent contexts of the passages in which it occurs: soldiers slaughtering all the males in a particular family group. Perpetrators of this kind of violence often denigrate and dehumanize their victims.

Paul and the Judaizers

We've focused so far on the Hebrew Bible, but the New Testament has some colorful passages as well. Take the book of Galatians. Paul is writing to Christians in the province of Galatia in eastern Turkey, and he's very upset with them. He foregoes the statement of praise for his readers that he usually includes at the beginning of his letters and instead expresses his astonishment that they have turned to "a different gospel." This different gospel is the teachings of "Judaizers," people who believe that Gentiles must accept Judaism in order to be Christians. Paul twice curses anyone who teaches a different gospel (Gal. 1:8, 9). The NRSV politely renders it, "Let that one be accursed." What Paul is really saying is, "Damn them!" This isn't profanity as one might use the term today. Paul is literally wishing eternal damnation on people he regards as heretics and enemies because of their teachings. He really means it.

The focal issue in the debate with the Judaizers is circumcision. The Judaizers teach that Gentiles converting to Christianity must undergo it. Paul strongly disagrees. In another letter, he calls the Judaizers "dogs" and refers to the practice of circumcision as mutilation (Phil. 3:2). Here in Galatians (5:12) he also expresses a wish that the Judaizers would mutilate themselves. The form of the verb he uses can refer to castration. This is undoubtedly what Paul means, and it is the way the NRSV translates. It is another indication of the bitterness Paul feels about this issue. Those who demand that Gentiles should remove their foreskins should just go ahead and cut off their own . . . well, fill in the blank.

Paul and His Accomplishments

One of the reasons that Paul so vehemently opposed the demand for circumcision is that before becoming a Christian he was a Jew. In fact, he was a devout leader of the Jews who persecuted Christians. (For the story of his conversion see Acts 9.) The change was remarkable. It also meant that he had to give up a lot, basically everything he had believed and followed and worked for. In his letter to the Philippians, a few verses after where he calls circumcision mutilation, Paul lists his attributes and accomplishments in his former life. He then says that compared to what he has gained in Christ, he regards all of his accomplishments, and in fact everything else in life, as worthless (Phil. 3:8). Actually, he puts it a little stronger than that. Most English translations use the words "rubbish" or "refuse." But the word Paul uses actually means "excrement." Again, the King James Version is more literal: it has "dung." Some translators have suggested that an appropriate rendering might be "shit." While Paul's word probably did not have the same connotation of profanity as "shit" has in English today, it does drive home the powerful feelings that Paul is voicing about his view of life outside of Christ. Just one more word you never expected to find in the Bible.

Where in the World?

Remember map quizzes in high school (maybe in college too)? You sit and memorize a bunch of strange names and where to locate them on an unlabeled map, which means drawing dots between meandering lines that are supposed to represent rivers and boundaries of countries, continents, and oceans. Later, though, you might read about one of those places in a novel or a history book and you suddenly want to understand where it is and what's around it. You may even decide to go and see this place for yourself, so now its location becomes even more interesting. And once you've visited a place, reading about it in a story or a newspaper suddenly takes on new meaning. This place isn't just a dot on a page any more but a part of your life and experience.

Even if you don't actually travel some place, though, a map can be crucial for understanding stories and history. Take *The Lord of the Rings*, the great trilogy and sequel to *The Hobbit*, by J.R.R. Tolkein, for example. If you haven't read it you probably at least saw the film version by Peter Jackson. The books all begin with a map of Middle Earth, and a map is displayed periodically during the course of the movies. You can't travel to Middle Earth, of course, because it's fictional. But it's important for the story to be able to trace the movements of the characters and events—Frodo and Sam as they approach Mount Doom, and the routes of different armies that converge for battle.

That's the way it is with the Bible too. We wish we could take you on a trip to visit the places that it mentions. (We suggested to the good people at Anselm Academic Press that offering a free tour of the Holy Land to everyone who bought a copy of this book would really boost sales, but they didn't think it would be cost-effective.) But whether you actually visit the lands of the Bible or not, a map is crucial for reading many of the Bible's stories. Sometimes consulting a map simply enriches the point of a particular episode. It can even transform your understanding of what is going on in the narrative.

In this chapter, we'll be discussing some Bible texts where geography is important. The chapter has two parts. In the first part we'll discuss some cases where just looking at a map sheds light on what is going on in a particular story or book. Our starting point is the story of King David, whom the Bible regards as the founder of the state of Israel and its greatest king. We will then look at the geography behind the book of Judges and some prophetic writings (Amos and Isaiah). In the second part, we'll probe a bit deeper and show how some familiarity with topography—in addition to the use of a map—enriches and clarifies some well-known Bible stories. In particular, we'll talk about the story of Sodom and Gomorrah in Genesis and a couple of famous New Testament stories: the demoniac named "Legion," and the "Good Samaritan."

Places and Plots: Knowing Where You Are Helps You See What It Means

GEOGRAPHY AND THE CHARACTER OF DAVID

David's predecessor, according to 1 Samuel, was King Saul. They had a "love-hate" relationship. That is, Saul loved David at first and then became jealous of him and grew to fear and hate him (1 Sam. 16–18). In fact, most of the story of David in 1 Samuel is about him evading Saul, who is out to kill him. Saul is from the tribe of Benjamin, David from Judah. A glance at a map shows that the lands of the two tribes were contiguous. Later on, after the death of Solomon, David's son and successor, Israel and Judah will split into separate countries, with the tribe of Benjamin actually joining Judah and David's heirs ruling the kingdom of Judah for the entirety of its history. Again, the map shows that David's

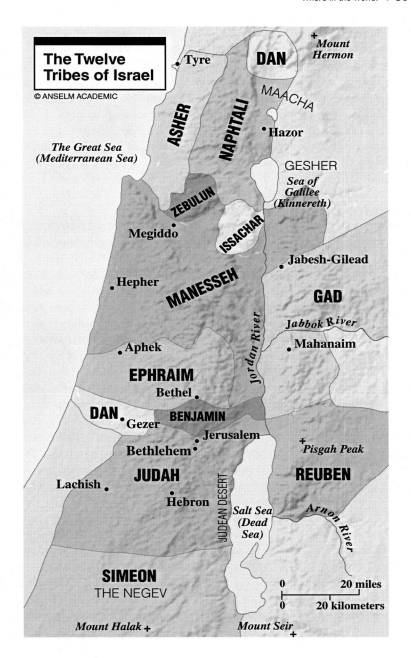

The Twelve Tribes of Israel

© ANSELM ACADEMIC

Tyre

DAN

+ *Mount Hermon*

MAACHA

ASHER

NAPHTALI

Hazor

The Great Sea (Mediterranean Sea)

GESHER

Sea of Galilee (Kinnereth)

ZEBULUN

Megiddo

ISSACHAR

Jabesh-Gilead

Hepher

MANESSEH

GAD

Jabbok River

Jordan River

Mahanaim

Aphek

EPHRAIM

Bethel

DAN *Gezer*   BENJAMIN

Jerusalem

+ *Pisgah Peak*

Bethlehem

JUDAH

REUBEN

Lachish

Hebron

JUDEAN DESERT

Salt Sea (Dead Sea)

Arnon River

SIMEON

THE NEGEV

0   20 miles

0   20 kilometers

Mount Halak +

Mount Seir +

hometown of Bethlehem was less than ten miles as the crow flies from Saul's hometown of Gibeah.

According to 1 Samuel 31, Saul was killed in battle against the Philistines on Mount Gilboa, overlooking the Jezreel Valley quite a distance north of Gibeah. His corpse was rescued and buried by the people of Jabesh-Gilead. There is an interesting narrative thread associated with Jabesh that involves its geographical location and that is important for understanding the story of David. Jabesh was in the region of Gilead east of the Jordan River in the territory that is now northern Jordan. Jabesh first comes up at the end of 1 Samuel 10 in a verse that was accidentally left out of the Hebrew Bible and can now be restored thanks to a Dead Sea Scrolls fragment.

The restored verse introduces the story in chapter 11. According to it, an Ammonite king named Nahash was oppressing Israelites in the tribes of Reuben and Gad, who lived east of the Jordan south of Jabesh. This was disputed territory that was claimed by both Israel and Ammon. Nahash was asserting his ownership of it and was marking the Israelites who lived in it as his subjects by gouging out their right eyes. Some of the Israelites in the disputed territory escaped and fled to Jabesh, which was really outside of the disputed region. But since some of his intended victims fled there, Nahash pursued them and besieged the city. The people of Jabesh talked Nahash into letting them seek a rescuer in Israel proper, i.e., west of the Jordan. If no one came to their aid, they would surrender to him. Apparently, Nahash was confident that no one would respond, saving him the trouble of having to take Jabesh by force. However, as 1 Samuel 11 describes, Saul did respond. His rescue of Jabesh earned him the throne over Israel and the gratitude of the city's population. When Saul died in battle, people of Jabesh rescued his body as a way of repaying their debt to him for rescuing them from Nahash and saving their right eyes.

After Saul died, his uncle, Abner, who commanded the army, installed Saul's son Ishbaal as king (2 Sam. 2:8–9). A comparison of these two verses with a map suggests the fragility of the kingdom following the defeat at Mount Gilboa. Ishbaal is made king over the regions of Gilead, Ashur (probably read "Geshur"), Jezreel, Ephraim, Benjamin, and "all Israel." In other words, he claimed significant territory on both sides of the Jordan. But Mahanaim, where Abner brought Ishbaal to make him king, was on the eastern side of the Jordan. Since there is no evidence of any tradition of coronation in Mahanaim, this suggests that the Philistines had taken control of most of Israel on the west side of the Jordan and that Ishbaal's hold on this territory was so tenuous that he could not even be crowned there. Later on in Samuel, we learn that the area around Mahanaim was thickly forested so as to make it easily defensible (2 Sam. 18:8), and this was likely another reason that Abner moved Ishbaal there.

The weakness of what had been Saul's kingdom and Ishbaal's hold on it probably also explains why David chose this time to make his move to replace Saul as king. The Bible simply reports an opening battle (2 Sam. 2:12–32) followed by the notice that there was a long civil war between David and his followers from Judah on the one hand and those loyal to Saul's family—especially the Benjaminites—on the other (2 Sam. 3:1). What precipitated the conflict may have been David's letter to the people of Jabesh-Gilead (2 Sam. 2:4b–7). After blessing them for their loyalty to Saul, he called on them to give their loyalty to him as the recently anointed king of Judah. The letter represented a threat and challenge to Ishbaal. David was trying to woo an enclave of strong support for Saul to himself. On top of that, the map shows that David was seeking to squeeze Ishbaal in a kind of pincers move. Ishbaal would be trapped between David to the south in Jerusalem and Jabesh to the north. To make matters worse, David's marriage to the daughter of the king of Geshur (2 Sam. 3:3) suggests that he may have had a treaty with that kingdom, again to the north of Mahanaim. Plus David was on good terms with at least one of the Philistine kings (Achish, 1 Sam. 27:1–28:2) who had overrun Ishbaal's kingdom. In short, David had Ishbaal cut off and effectively surrounded. Ishbaal's only option was to go on the offensive against David in order to try to win back some of his territory.

All of this—namely the significance of Jabesh-Gilead and Mahanaim—becomes clear from a consideration of the story with a map. In a real sense, consulting a map offers a different slant on David from a surface reading of the story, indicating that David was not just a naive lad who happened into leadership by luck or divine choice. Rather, the map suggests that he was an ambitious politician and a clever military strategist.

GEOGRAPHY AND THE THEOLOGY OF JUDGES

Moving backwards in the Bible from David and the beginning of the monarchy in 1–2 Samuel, we return to the book of Judges. To recap, the "major" judges, who have stories about them, in order of appearance in the book and with the tribes they are from, are: Othniel of Judah, Ehud of Benjamin, Deborah of Ephraim, Gideon of Manasseh, Jephthah of Gilead, and Samson of Dan. It is striking, first of all, that the judges all come from different tribes. A glance at a map shows that this order of tribes reflects a progression from south to north. Judah was the southernmost tribe, Dan the northernmost.[1] The tribe directly to the north of Judah was Benjamin, followed by Ephraim, then Manasseh. With Manasseh the list crosses the Jordan, since Manasseh had two parts, one on either side of the Jordan. Gilead was also east of the Jordan. Dan was at the sources of the Jordan.

It seems unlikely that this progression is due to coincidence. Rather, it reflects the way in which the book of Judges was put together. But this has implications for our understanding of history. The book presents the time of the judges as a period in Israel's history after the conquest but before the monarchy when the nation of Israel was ruled by charismatic figures. The arrangement of the stories according to a geographical pattern, though, suggests that this was not their historical order. Instead, they seem to be tales emerging from different tribes. In other words, they were local heroes, not national ones. The author(s) or editor(s) of the book presented them as national figures for theological reasons, in order to represent the time of the judges as a period in Israel's history in which the nation went through a repeated cycle of sin, punishment, repentance, and rescue. The lesson for readers was that whenever Israel was in crisis, God would rescue them if they would repent and call on him. Geography signals theology.

TARGET PRACTICE: AMOS'S ORACLES AGAINST THE NATIONS

Amos was a prophet in the eighth century BCE who came from Judah but worked in Israel. He focused on Israel's social injustices,

---

[1] Judges 18 contains a story about the migration of the Danites from the south to the north. However, by the time the book was edited into its present form Dan was firmly established in the north. Simeon was absorbed into Judah at a relatively early date.

such as the mistreatment of the poor, and as a result is a favorite of people concerned with social justice today. For example, Dr. Martin Luther King, Jr., often quoted Amos in his sermons and speeches. You will probably recognize Amos 5:24 as one of those quotations from his famous "I Have a Dream" speech: "But let justice roll down like waters, and righteousness like an ever-flowing stream."

The book of Amos begins (chs. 1–2), though, not with an oracle against Israel but with a series of oracles against other nations. Now, it is not unusual for prophetic books to have a section of oracles against other nations; Isaiah, Jeremiah, and Ezekiel all have such a section. What is unusual about Amos is that the book actually begins with these oracles, even though other nations were not Amos's primary concern.

The nations that are addressed are Syria or Aram, represented by Damascus (Amos 1:3–5), the Philistines (1:6–8), Tyre and the Phoenicians (1:9–10), Edom (1:11–12), Ammon (1:13–15), Moab (2:1–3), and finally Judah (2:4–5), followed by Israel (2:6–11 or 6–16). If you look at a map, you'll see that these nations were Israel's neighbors pretty much all around. Syria was (and is) east-northeast, the Philistines southwest, Tyre and Phoencians north, Edom southeast, Ammon and Moab east-southeast, and Judah due south. The fact that the last oracle in this collection is directed against Israel itself suggests that the book is pinpointing places all around just to focus its energy on Israel. It's like drawing a target; the nations all around are the outer rings, but Israel is the bull's-eye.

This impression is furthered by subsequent materials in the book. Amos 3:2, for instance, says, "You only have I known of all the families of the earth; therefore I will punish you for all your iniquities." In other words, Israel was the only people with whom God had a special relationship going back to the Exodus from Egypt (2:10; 3:1), so they were held to a higher standard of behavior than the other nations. More was expected of Israel because of their closeness to God, so the punishment for their social failings was to be more exacting.

Israel's special relationship to God in contrast to the nations may also lie behind the theme of the "day of the LORD" in Amos. You can imagine the Israelites cheering at the oracles against the other nations, who were their neighbors but also their rivals and sometimes their enemies. They think of the "day of the LORD" as some point when Yahweh will bring destruction and punishment on those foreigners for their attacks and offenses against his people, Israel. But Amos 5:18 says, "Alas for you who desire the day of the LORD. . . . It is darkness not light." The point seems to be that Yahweh is coming in judgment, and he will punish the nations. But his real target is his own people, Israel, who form the geographic center of Amos's prophecies.

THE WAY HOME: RETURN FROM EXILE

The large book of Isaiah is actually two or even three books put together. The first thirty-nine chapters contain materials that go back to the eighth-century prophet who lent his name to the book. Beginning in chapter 40, though, the setting of the oracles changes to 539–538 BCE. In 539 the Persian king Cyrus conquered Babylon and established a new empire. Isaiah 44:28 and 45:1 presuppose this event when they mention Cyrus as Yahweh's anointed, who is commissioned to release the people of Judah from captivity so that they can return home to rebuild the temple in Jerusalem. Throughout chapters 40–55 this return is envisioned as a glorious procession from Babylon to Jerusalem led by Yahweh himself. For instance, 40:2 says that Jerusalem has paid for its sins and 40:3–4 describes God lowering mountains and raising valleys in order to create a straight, easy road for the people to walk on as they travel home. A similar image is found in 45:2a and 49:11. In 48:20, they are told to go out from Babylon and in 52:11 to depart. The ruins of Jerusalem are called upon to break into singing to welcome them back (52:9).

The map makes clear that there was and is indeed a wilderness, as Isaiah 40:3 suggests, between Babylon and Jerusalem. In fact, it was and is a large desert—a section of the modern country of Saudi Arabia. The usual route of travel and trade in antiquity was to avoid the desert and to follow the cultivatable area known as the "Fertile Crescent." Hence, someone going from Babylon to Jerusalem would typically travel northwest first and then south. In that sense, the vision of the second part of Isaiah is highly unrealistic. In fact, it is not meant to be realistic at all. It is a vision, an ideal, meant to inspire

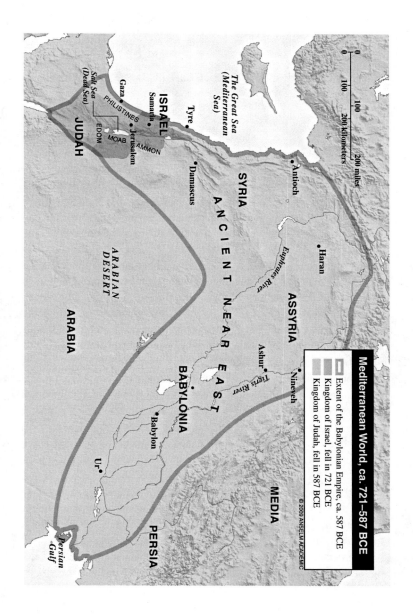

Mediterranean World, ca. 721–587 BCE

☐ Extent of the Babylonian Empire, ca. 587 BCE
▨ Kingdom of Israel, fell in 721 BCE
▨ Kingdom of Judah, fell in 587 BCE

© 2009 ANSELM ACADEMIC

hope for the future, reassurance of God's guidance and protection. It is inspirational and celebratory literature, not an actual travel guide or itinerary. Here, geography aids in the appreciation of the literary genre and animating poetry of "Second Isaiah" (chs. 40–55).

The Lay of the Land: Geographical Formations Inform Biblical Tales

LOT'S LEGACY

The story in Genesis 19 is one of the most misinterpreted in the Bible, and it's largely due to a lack of familiarity with topography. The story actually begins back in chapter 13, where Abraham (there called Abram) and Lot have become so wealthy that their shepherds have taken to quarreling. Abram offers Lot a sweet deal—his choice of whatever part of the land he wishes, so that the two of them can split up and stop the fighting. Lot, selfishly or sensibly, chooses the "plain of the Jordan" because it is lush and well-watered. This "plain of the Jordan" is the Jordan Valley, specifically the section around the southern end of the Dead Sea, as shown by the mention of Sodom and Gomorrah in 13:10. The story assumes that the entire Jordan Valley, including the Dead Sea, and perhaps even further south was once green and fertile, just as it is today between the Sea of Galilee and the Dead Sea.

Of course, a quick image search on Google reveals that the area around the Dead Sea, especially its southern end, is anything but fertile and lush today. And it never was, at least not as long as humans have roamed the planet. The story about how it got to be the way it is today is in Genesis 19. It is an etiology, a story—typically fanciful rather than historical in nature—that explains how something came to be. In this case, the story in Genesis 19 explains how that region around the Dead Sea came to be so hot and desolate: God rained fire and sulfur (brimstone) on it. The sulfur accounts for the odor around the Dead Sea resulting from the mineral content left after evaporation, since the water has no outlet. The mineral formations that sometimes result are reflected in the anecdote about Lot's wife turning into a pillar of salt. Even the name of the city of Zoar (meaning "small") is etiological, as the puns in 19:20–22 indicate.

The story also ends with an etiology that explains the origins of the Ammonites and Moabites, the peoples on the other side of the Dead Sea from Israel (modern Jordan). In one of the lewdest tales in the Bible, Lot's daughters conspire to seduce him. The resulting sons are named Moab and Ben-Ammi, the eponymous ancestors, respectively, of the Moabites and Ammonites.

Now, on the basis of the best historical, archeological, and geographic evidence, the story appears to have no basis in actual events. The features of the Dead Sea and its environs are the result of geological formations. The deep rift valley allows no egress to the water flowing in from the Jordan, so that the accumulated water can only evaporate, leaving behind the minerals it has borne downstream. The incest in the story at the end was suggested by the names "Moab" and "Ammon," the former being similar to Hebrew "from father" (*me'ab*) and the latter to "people" (*'am*). Hence, Ben-Ammi means "son of my people." Of course, the story also served to disparage these neighbors and sometime rivals or enemies of Israel by identifying them as, in effect, a bunch of incestuous bastards. Given that the ancient Israelites were not supposed to intermarry with the Moabites and Ammonites, the story of their origin offers another good reason for not doing so.

Geography and topography are important for seeing what this story is really up to. It is worth noting that understanding what the story is really about raises serious doubts about using it—as is commonly done—to condemn homosexuality. The etiological nature of the story shows that its concerns relate to the geographical, political, and cultural setting of ancient Israel and have nothing to do with things like sexual orientation in modern society. To be sure, in the story, God has a moral reason for destroying the area of Sodom and Gomorrah. That reason is their citizens' mistreatment of visitors, dominating them by violence and gang rape, which again have nothing to do with sexual orientation as we understand it today. The history of interpretation of this passage serves as a cautionary tale not to read our own assumptions and issues into the biblical text.

LEGION'S DEMONS

Considerations of geography and topography also suggest that a lot more is going on behind the story of the demoniac Legion in the Gospel of Mark. The story is well known. Jesus crosses over the Sea of Galilee in the middle of the night, stilling a storm (Mark 4:35–41). On the other side, he encounters a man filled with demons whose name is Legion. Jesus casts the demons out of him into a herd of swine grazing nearby. The swine then rush into the sea and drown.

Palestine at the Time of Jesus

© 2009 ANSELM ACADEMIC

Sidon

Damascus

SYRIA

+ Mt. Hermon

Tyre

PHOENICIA

Caesarea Philippi

The Great Sea
(Mediterranean Sea)

GALILEE

Capernaum · Bethsaida

Magdala · Sea of Galilee (Kinnereth)

Mt. Carmel + Cana · Gergesa

Sepphoris Tiberias

Nazareth + Gedara

+ Mt. Tabor

DECAPOLIS

Caesarea
Maritima

SAMARIA

Gerasa

Jordan River

Mt. Gerizim + Sychar

Joppa

Arimathea?

PEREA

Emmaus? Jericho

Jerusalem + Mt. Olives

Bethany

JUDEA

Salt
Sea
(Dead
Sea)

Hebron

IDUMEA

0   20   40 mi

0   20   40 kilometers

A major problem presented by the story is where it is supposed to have taken place. Mark locates it in the "country of the Gerasenes." Gerasa was the site of the modern-day ruins of Jerash, one of the best preserved of the Roman provincial cities from the time of Jesus. You will be surprised, once you locate it on a map, to see how far away it is from the Sea of Galilee—close to forty miles as the crow flies. That's quite a distance for a herd of stampeding pigs to run. The ancient writers and copyists recognized the problem. That's why Matthew (8:28) and some manuscripts of Mark locate the story near Gedara (modern Um Qeis), still several miles away, or Gergesa (probably modern Kursi, on the shore of the Sea of Galilee). But if the story was originally set at one of these other places, why would Mark or a later copyist relocate it to a place that was farther away and made less sense? The reason may lie in the name "Legion." The name may be an allusion to the Roman 10th Legion, which put down the Jewish revolt of 70 CE, destroying Jerusalem in the process, and which appears to have been stationed briefly in Gerasa following 70. It even used the boar as one of its standards. Mark may have told this story in order to make a subtle political and theological point—that the Roman army was demonic but that God would destroy them as he had destroyed Pharaoh and the Egyptians by throwing them into the sea and rescuing his people. The former demoniac, who is probably a Gentile to judge from the fact that he is living in a predominantly Gentile area where pigs are herded, is sent home to tell his friends and neighbors about Jesus (vv. 19–20), hinting at the acceptance of Gentiles into the future Christian community. Again, careful consideration of geography and topography reveals theology.

THE "GOOD SAMARITAN"

The famous story told by Jesus in Luke 10:30–36 is set on the road between Jerusalem and Jericho. This was a stretch of about seventeen miles in which the altitude drops more than 3,000 feet. That's because Jerusalem sits on a mountain, about 2,500 feet above sea level, while Jericho, just north of the Dead Sea, the lowest place on the globe, was some 800 feet below sea level. The rainwater rushing downhill over the millennia had carved deep ravines, known as wadis, in the terrain. As a result, the route between these two cities was rugged and notorious for dangers from bandits. Its infamy is probably why Jesus chose it for his story. It might be comparable to walking alone in a high-crime neighborhood of a modern American city.

Another important piece of background for understanding this story was the animosity that existed between Jews and Samaritans. No hatred is as intense as that which can be found between brothers. Samaritans and Jews were alike in many ways. Both worshipped the same God. Both regarded the Law of Moses as sacred scripture. They shared common history. There were even blood ties between them. But the Jews regarded the Samaritans as ethnically perverted and religiously illegitimate, and the Samaritans returned the compliment. The hatred between them was so bad that Jews often avoided Samaria when traveling to the Galilee region. That meant crossing the Jordan and traveling north on the other side of it before crossing back over once they had passed Samaria—quite a detour. Samaritans reciprocated by showing some hospitality to those traveling away from Jerusalem but refusing it for those traveling toward it. The man in the story might even be thought of as on his way to Jericho in order to cross the Jordan and thus avoid Samaria.

The priest and Levite in the story probably avoid the injured man for religious reasons. They apparently think he is dead and do not want to touch him lest they become ritually unclean. It is the Samaritan, who would be expected to be least sympathetic to the man, who actually shows him mercy. The point Jesus seems to be making by telling the story this way is that the Samaritan's kindness and acts of mercy trump the religious scruples of the priest and Levite—scruples that, in and of themselves, are perfectly appropriate and right.

An understanding of the topography and geography help to make the story realistic. While the story is often referred to today as the Parable of the Good Samaritan, neither Jesus nor Luke refers to it this way. Of course, it might well be a parable. It is a story designed to make a point or teach a lesson, which is what parables are. Simply launching into the story and not referring to it as a parable, however, emphasizes its realism; it was something that could and did happen commonly. Knowing the topography reinforces this realism and makes the question, "Which of these three was a neighbor to the man?" and the final instruction, "Go and do likewise," all the more pointed and forceful.

8 All in a Name

The Name Game

Names are often a source of fascination and amusement. What we call ourselves, our offspring, the places we inhabit, and the things around us can intrigue, entertain, or repel. Think about the last time you met someone with an unusual name or drove past a road sign for a place like Intercourse, Pennsylvania—see, you know what we're talking about. There wouldn't be an annual list of most popular baby names if people weren't captivated by the topic.

The extent of our interest in names—the fancy term for the study of names is *onomastics*—is easy to verify. An internet search on Amazon using the phrase "meanings of names" turns up 625 titles, covering an amaz(on)ing range of topics. There are books on first names, last names, place-names, plant names, planet names, pets' names, pet names, nicknames, brand names, bird names, railway station names, and pub names (that one must have entailed some fun research). Other works treat African names, Irish names, Iowa names, God's names, Jewish names, Christian names, Muslim names, and Hindu names. There's even a book titled *The Origin and Meaning of the Name Yggdrasill* that's only thirteen pages long and discusses the name of a large tree that's important in Norse mythology.

It's impossible to know all the causes behind people's interest in names, but it's quite likely that the Bible has had some influence. In the biblical literature names play a key role in many stories associated with some of the best-known figures in the text. There are certain formulas and stock scenes that are associated with the ritual of naming a child, and often the meanings associated with those names factor into the plot. Elsewhere, adults are sometimes given a new name that signals a change in identity or status that has a bearing on how a story unfolds. Similarly, place-names are frequently mentioned in the Bible, and they sometimes function in unusual and unexpected ways. In some cases, there are marvelous puns and wordplays in biblical names that are totally lost when translated into another language like English. Because the Bible has played such a formative role in people's lives it's easy to believe that its careful attention to names has had a bearing on how we relate to names in our daily lives. That might explain why so many of those 625 books mentioned above deal explicitly with names in the Bible.

The present chapter explores this aspect of names in the biblical material. Phonebooks didn't exist in antiquity, of course, but imagine discovering one from biblical times. As we thumb through its pages and pause over some of the names of people and places, what might we learn about them? As is often the case with the Bible, the answer will likely surprise you.

A Bitter/Sweet Story

We begin by considering the book of Ruth; the work is set in the period of the Judges before Israel was a kingdom, but it was probably written at a much later time. This book describes the story of a woman named Ruth, who was from the land of Moab on the opposite side of the Dead Sea from Israel in the modern country of Jordan. Ruth married into a family from Bethlehem that had fled to Moab to escape a famine that threatened their land. The family was comprised of a couple, named Elimelech and Naomi, and their two sons, Mahlon and Chilion. One by one, the males in the family died, first Elimelech and then his two sons. After their father's death the brothers had married Ruth and Orpah, two women from among the local population. But the marriages did not produce children, so when Naomi's two sons passed away the family had been reduced to three widows, Naomi and her two Moabite daughters-in-law.

When Naomi learns that the famine in Israel is over, she decides to return to her people in Bethlehem. She convinces Orpah to remain in Moab, but Ruth opts instead to go to Judah with her mother-in-law. Once the two women arrive there Ruth plays a key role in restoring Naomi's status and reputation in Bethlehem, primarily through having a child with a man named Boaz who is a relative of Naomi's deceased husband Elimelech. Much of the action in the story describes the twists and turns in the relationship between Ruth and Boaz—how they meet, hook up, and eventually marry. A somewhat ambiguous episode takes place in the third chapter of the book that many scholars think portrays a steamy scene on a threshing floor in which Ruth seduces an intoxicated Boaz.

A central theme of the book of Ruth is universality, particularly the idea that God's presence and involvement are not limited to the land and people of Israel. Ruth is the quintessential outsider, and the book never lets the reader forget that fact because it regularly refers to her as "the Moabite." Despite her foreign status she is instrumental in enabling Naomi's family line to continue due to a custom known as "levirate marriage." This practice was an ancient form of sperm donorship that had important legal implications. When a man died childless, one of his male relatives could marry the widow, and if any children were born of the union they were legally considered to be the heirs of the deceased man. In this way, the baby conceived by Ruth and Boaz was considered to be Naomi's grandson.

But Obed was no ordinary baby, as his birth had a significant bearing on the future of the Israelite people. The book of Ruth ends with a listing of his genealogy, including his grandson David, whom the Bible celebrates as the greatest king of Israel. In other words, David's great-grandmother was Ruth, a foreigner without a drop of Israelite blood, who was from Moab, whose inhabitants are often presented in the Bible as the enemies par excellence of the Israelites. This is a very inclusive view of foreign peoples, and it's one of the reasons why many scholars think the book of Ruth reached its final form at a relatively late date. It challenges the many passages elsewhere in the Hebrew Bible that privilege Israelites over others who are not considered to be worthy of membership among the people of God. For our purposes, perhaps the most noteworthy of these passages is Deuteronomy 23:3a. "No Ammonite or Moabite shall be admitted to the assembly of the LORD. Even to the tenth generation, none of their descendants shall be admitted to the assembly of the LORD." It's hard to reconcile that with how the book of Ruth ends, since it presents David as a third-generation descendant of a Moabite.

Like many other characters in the Bible, Naomi is really tuned in to the meanings of names. When she returns to Bethlehem with Ruth in tow and the local women ask, "Is this Naomi?" her response is a curious one. "Call me no longer Naomi, call me Mara, for the Almighty has dealt bitterly with me" (1:20). In its English translation the point she is making can go right over our heads unless we have some knowledge of biblical Hebrew or a Bible with explanatory footnotes (and we read them). Naomi rejects her given name because it means "pleasant" or "sweet," which is not how she feels after the death of her husband and sons. Rather, she believes God has abandoned her—in her words, "the Almighty has dealt bitterly with me"—and so she renames herself Mara, which literally means "bitter."

She continues to be called Naomi throughout the book, however, so her comment doesn't signal a real name change. It functions more as a pun or expression of despair that reflects her awareness that her name doesn't fit her present circumstances. Interestingly, the women of the town return at the end of the book when they celebrate the birth of the child. As she holds him to her bosom the women cry out, "A son has been born to Naomi" (4:17). Here and in the first chapter, when they ask, "Is this Naomi?" are the only two places in the book where someone else calls her by name in her presence. But this time she doesn't reject her name and suggest that she be called Mara instead, as she did earlier. Now the name fits and Naomi's double reversal of fortune is complete. She's gone from "sweet" to "bitter" and back to "sweet" again, thanks to a foreign daughter-in-law who stayed with her.

Naomi is not the only member of her family whose name provides information about its bearer. The most interesting examples are her sons Mahlon and Chilion, whose names mean "sickly" and "weak" respectively. This is the author's way of letting us know that these guys aren't going to be around for long. To the ancient Israelite reader the significance would have been readily apparent, just as a modern reader immediately gets the implications of the name "Pigpen" assigned to the hopelessly dirty character in Charles M. Schulz's *Peanuts* comic strip. But, once again, the only way a modern reader can be in on the biblical joke about Mahlon and Chilion is to somehow know the meanings of the Hebrew words that identify the brothers.

Elimelech's name is less clever or indicative of some quality he possesses, but it still has a meaning. It translates as "my God is king," and it is one of many personal names in the Bible that contain the *El* prefix and are actually statements about God. Other examples include Elijah ("my God is Yahweh"), Eliab ("my God is father"), Elihu ("he is my God"), and Eliezer ("my God is help"). The *El* prefix is an example of what scholars refer to as a "theophoric element" that describes some aspect or action of a deity. Another very common one in the Bible is *Yah*, which is often a shortened form of Yahweh. It's found in the name Elijah, mentioned above, which is composed of two theophoric elements, the second of which is often transliterated into English as "Jeho" or "Jo." Examples of names that contain this element include Jehoiakim ("Yahweh has established"), Jonathan ("Yahweh has given"), Joshua ("Yahweh saves"), and Jehoshaphat ("Yahweh has judged").

Boaz's name means something like "in him is strength," and scholars are divided over whether it is meant to be a reference to his physical might or intellectual acumen. In favor of the latter alternative is a scene in chapter 4 in which he outwits another relative of Naomi's husband who would like to have the family's land but doesn't want Ruth who comes along with it. By the way, that man remains unnamed in the story but Boaz refers to him using an unusual Hebrew phrase that might have the sense of "so-and-so" or "what's-his-face." Coincidentally, Boaz is also the name of one of the bronze pillars that stood in front of Solomon's temple (1 Kings 7:21–22).

The book is named after Ruth and she is its main character, but scholars do not agree about the meaning of her name. Some have suggested it might be a form of the Hebrew term that describes a female companion but, like other suggestions that have been proposed, that idea has not met widespread support. The same thing holds for Orpah's name, but in this case there's an interesting pop culture connection. Careful readers will note that her name looks very similar to that of a certain iconic television talk-show personality. In fact, Oprah Winfrey was supposed to have been named after Orpah in the book of Ruth but two of the letters were transposed on her birth certificate. It was probably her first good career move because if it had been spelled correctly the name of her production company would have been Hapro instead of the easier-on-the-ear Harpo.[1]

To wrap up the discussion of names in Ruth we'll briefly treat two of the places mentioned in the book: Moab and Bethlehem. The precise meaning of the word *Moab* is debated by scholars, but the Bible offers an etymology of sorts toward the end of the well-known Sodom and Gomorrah story in Genesis 19. After those cities are destroyed Lot flees to the hills with his two daughters. Thinking they are the only people to survive the conflagration, the two women decide to get their father drunk and have sex with him in order to perpetuate the human race. The chapter concludes by mentioning that the names of the two sons born of these unions were Moab and Ben-ammi, who were the ancestors of the Moabites and the Ammonites.

There is some major biblical trash-talking going on here. By identifying the Moabites and the Ammonites as the product of incest, this story insults and belittles two neighboring peoples with whom the Israelites were often in conflict. It traces them to two individuals whose very names hint at their shameful origins. Ben-ammi, literally "son of my people," can be interpreted as a pun that pokes fun at how the Ammonite family line got its start, and the same can be said about Moab. It is very similar to the Hebrew phrase that means "from father," and it echoes what Lot's older daughter twice says to the younger when she urges that they "preserve offspring through [lit. "from"] our father" (Gen. 19:32, 34).

The meaning of the name "Bethlehem" is much tamer by comparison. The Bible actually mentions more than one town bearing this name. In addition to the one in Judah from Ruth, there is one in Zebulun (Josh. 19:15) and another mentioned in Judges (12:8–10) that might or might not be the same as the one listed in Joshua. It is, of course, celebrated by Christians as the birthplace of Jesus, but Bethlehem was first associated with King David. In fact, many Bible scholars believe the tradition that Jesus was born in Bethlehem stems from its connection with David since it was commonly held that the Messiah would come from the line of David. The name Bethlehem translates as "house of bread," and no compelling theories have been

---

[1] It says something, we're not sure what, that the spell-check feature of our software accepts the spelling of Oprah, but not that of Orpah.

put forward regarding what the name might mean. Several place-names in the Bible begin with the Hebrew word for "house," with one of the most prominent being Bethel ("house of God"). As its name suggests, a "house" might be a temple, and Bethlehem might mean "temple of (the god of) war," since the words for *war* and *bread* are similar in Hebrew.

Baby Formula

Sometimes, as in the case of Mara, the meanings of names in the Bible are explicitly mentioned in the text. This is usually found in a birth scene that typically has three parts: mention of the birth of a child, the child is given a name, the meaning of the name is stated or implied. This formula is sometimes modified in small ways, but the outline is normally followed quite closely. For example, in a few cases God or an angel announces the birth of the child or tells the father or mother what the child's name will be.

With two exceptions—Jesus and John the Baptist—all of these birth narratives are found in the Hebrew Bible, and most of them explain the names of important people who either play a prominent role in the text or are significant for the Israelite community. The very first birth recorded in the Bible contains a modified version of the formula. When Cain is born, Eve says, "I have produced a man with the help of the LORD" (Gen. 4:1). Although the connection between the name and what she says isn't apparent in English, the Hebrew word translated "produced" is similar to Cain's name and thus serves to explain its origin. Even though it is not in a birth story, there is a reference to the meaning of Eve's name in Genesis 3:20, which explains that she bears this name because "she was the mother of all living," drawing on the similarity between the Hebrew words for "Eve" and "living."

The full pattern begins to emerge with the births of Abraham's two sons. When Ishmael, whose name means "God hears," is conceived, an angel appears to his mother Hagar and informs her that she is to call her son by that name because "the LORD has given heed to your affliction" (Gen. 16:11). Isaac's name means "he laughs," and laughter is a common theme in texts that treat his conception and birth. When he is born, his mother Sarah remarks, "God has brought laughter for me; everyone who hears will laugh with me" (Gen. 21:6). Similarly, when she first learns of her pregnancy she laughs and is reprimanded by God (Gen. 18:9–15).

Isaac's sons Esau and Jacob provide an interesting example because they are twins (Gen. 25:24–26). In an impressive display of sibling rivalry that is a sign of things to come, they wrestle each other while still in the womb. The one born first is given the name Esau because he is red and covered with hair. The Hebrew words for "red" and "hair" are not etymologically related to Esau's name, but they are similar to the words for Edom and Seir, two places associated with the offspring of Esau. This passage therefore does not explain the meaning of Esau's name, but it establishes the connection between him and the area south of the Dead Sea.

Jacob is an unusual case because his name has two different meanings in Genesis. According to the birth narrative, he is given his name because when they were born he held on to his brother's heel, and the Hebrew term for "held on" comes from the same root as "Jacob." But two chapters later, after Jacob has stolen the blessing from their father Isaac that was meant for his twin brother, Esau says that Jacob is aptly named because he supplanted Esau. Here he is drawing on the basic meaning of the Hebrew root that means "to supplant, deceive."

The twelve sons of Jacob are the eponymous ancestors of the twelve tribes of Israel. Eponymy is when the name of a group or place is derived from that of an individual, like Washington D.C. or Disneyworld (some would say they're the same place). The birth stories of all twelve brothers contain the standard naming formula, complete with an explanation of each brother's name (Gen. 29:32–35; 30:4–13, 17–20, 22–23; 35:18). It is therefore quite striking that when Jacob's only daughter is born the text simply says, "Afterwards she (Leah) bore a daughter, and named her Dinah" (Gen. 30:21) and provides no information on what the name means. In fact, nowhere in the Bible is a daughter's name ever explained or elaborated upon. This is probably due to the fact that ancient Israelite culture was patriarchal, with lineage traced through the male side of the family. Consequently, the male ancestors attract the attention of the biblical authors.

Another well-known figure whose story includes the naming formula is Moses. In this case it appears not at the time of his birth but a bit later, when the child's mother returns him to Pharaoh's daughter, who names him Moses because "I drew him out of the water" (Exod. 2:10). There is a Hebrew root related to Moses' name that has this meaning ("to draw out"), but many scholars question why an Egyptian woman would give a Hebrew name to a boy she has taken as her own son. The Hebrew meaning might fit the events of the story, but it is more likely that Moses' name derives from an Egyptian verb that means "to give birth" and is found in other Egyptian names like Ramses, which means "Ra is born." Later in the same chapter Moses employs the naming formula on his son Gershom, whose name relates to Moses' experience as an alien (*ger*) in a foreign land (Exod. 2:22).

The most puzzling name explanation in the Bible involves Samuel in 1 Samuel 1:20. When his mother Hannah gives birth to him she names him Samuel because she "asked him of the LORD." The problem is that the name Samuel is unrelated to the Hebrew word for "asked" used here. Scholars continue to debate the precise meaning of Samuel's name, but senses related to "asking" are never mentioned. In all likelihood, we have a case of mistaken identity here. Saul will make his appearance in 1 Samuel a few chapters later, and his name *is* related to the Hebrew root that means "to ask." As the story unfolds there are several other wordplays and puns in the chapter that obviously relate to Saul's name, creating the impression that Saul, not Samuel, was the original birthday boy in the story (1 Sam. 1:17, 27, 28). Why all these allusions to Saul? The bottom line is that we don't know for sure. Perhaps it's the author's way of saying that the child is the father of the man. As an adult, King Saul will fall out of favor with God and be replaced by David, whom the biblical author considers to be the ideal ruler. Maybe the story of Samuel's birth is subtly anticipating those events. There is no birth story of Saul in the Bible, but there's a hint of one here when the infant Saul suffers the same fate as his grown self and is pushed aside in favor of the more popular Samuel.

The book of Isaiah contains a naming text that is quoted in the New Testament. Isaiah tries to encourage King Ahaz by telling him that God will give him a sign in the form of a newborn baby. "Look, the young woman is with child and shall bear a son, and shall name him Immanuel" (Isa. 7:14). This is not a complete naming formula because it lacks any reference to the name's meaning. But that missing element is added in Matthew's Gospel when the author cites the Isaiah text in reference to Jesus' conception and after the name Immanuel adds, "Which means, 'God is with us'" (Matt. 1:23).

Matthew's Gospel also contains the New Testament's best example of the naming formula a couple of verses before its citation of the Immanuel oracle. An angel appears to Joseph to reassure him that he should go on with his plans to wed Mary. "She will bear a son, and you are to name him Jesus, for he will save his people from their sins" (Matt. 1:21). Like the rest of the New Testament, Matthew's Gospel is written in Greek, but this verse reflects the author's familiarity with Hebrew since it is that form of Jesus' name (*yeshua*) that means "God saves."

Speaking of Jesus, we might be stating the obvious, but his last name wasn't "Christ." People in biblical times did not have family names that were passed down from generation to generation like today. Similar to the custom in some modern cultures, people were often identified in relation to who their father was. So, for example, the apostle Peter is sometimes referred to as "Simon, son of Jonah" (Matt. 16:17) or "Simon, son of John" (John 1:42). "Christ" is a transliteration of the Greek word *christos*, which means "anointed one." It is a translation of the Hebrew term *mashiah* that has the same meaning and is the basis for the English word *messiah*. Christ is therefore a title for Jesus and not a proper name. (And, just for the record, his middle initial wasn't "H.")

Biblical Aliases

Several characters in the Bible undergo name changes during their lifetimes that are more permanent than Naomi's suggestion that she be called Mara. They are typically renamed by someone in a position of authority over them, and the change in name signals a corresponding change in status. God changes Abram's name to Abraham in Genesis 17:5 in the middle of a scene in which a covenant is established between the two parties. The two names were probably just dialectical variants, but the author has invested them with special meaning. Abram, literally "exalted ancestor," has now become Abraham ("ancestor of a multitude"), and just prior to renaming him, God tells him he will be "the ancestor of a multitude of nations." Abraham's wife experiences a similar change when God says that Sarai's name will now be Sarah (Gen. 17:15). These are actually closely related names that both mean "princess," but the shift still represents a significant change in the character's status. The first time Sarai is mentioned in the Bible (Gen. 11:29–30) it is stated that she is childless, but immediately after her name change we are told that she will have a son and give rise to many peoples (Gen. 17:16). The double renaming highlights that it is impossible for Abram to become the ancestor of many unless Sarai becomes a mother.

Jacob's name change is the most significant in the Bible because he becomes Israel, the entire community's ancestor, whose sons give their names to the twelve tribes. This is another example of eponymy. In the case of Jacob, his name is changed after he has a weird wrestling match with what might be another person, an angel, or maybe even God. His opponent dubs him Israel because he has "striven with God and with humans and has prevailed" (Gen. 32:28). The verse's interpretation of the name has its basis in a Hebrew root found within it that means "to fight, contend." This is the first time that the word *Israel* appears in the biblical text.

There is another passage a couple of chapters later in which God changes Jacob's name to Israel, but the meaning of the name is not specified (Gen. 35:10). The covenant is not mentioned in this passage but there are some echoes of the scene of Abraham's name change mentioned above, including a promise from God that a company of nations will come from Jacob, a guarantee of offspring, and explicit mention of Abraham.

Another name change in the Hebrew Bible is the one Joseph undergoes in Genesis 41:45 when the Egyptian Pharaoh makes him a member of his court and gives him the name Zaphenath-paneah. It is easy to overlook this name change because it's mentioned in just this one verse and the character is still called "Joseph" throughout the remainder of the story, which isn't too surprising because Zaphenath-paneah is quite a mouthful. Nonetheless, it is an interesting example of the conventional pattern because, as with the other name changes seen so far, the change is initiated by one in a position of authority, only this time it is the Egyptian monarch rather than God. Unlike the others, though, Joseph undergoes a total makeover here as he also acquires a new wardrobe, jewelry, transportation, and a spouse (Gen. 41:41–45). Now that's an upgrade.

In the New Testament, the apostle Peter is the prime example of someone who has a name reassignment. His given name was Simon, but he is more commonly known as Peter, a name bestowed on him by Jesus. "And I tell you, you are Peter, and on this rock I will build my church, and the gates of Hades will not prevail against it" (Matt. 16:18; cf. Mark 3:16; John 1:42). Here, too, a pun is at work because the Greek word for "Peter" (*Petros*) is virtually identical to the one for "rock" (*petra*). Another name that Peter sometimes goes by in the New Testament is Cephas, which is the equivalent of both "Peter" and "rock" in Aramaic, the language spoken in Palestine during Jesus' lifetime (John 1:42). Here, as in other renaming passages, his new name indicates a change of status for Peter because Jesus is singling him out as the foundation upon which he will establish his community.

It is sometimes wrongly assumed that Paul also underwent a name change from Saul, but in fact, Paul/Saul appears to have used both names after his conversion, and possibly before. The Bible does not explain how he happens to go by two unrelated names. Saul is, of course, an old Hebrew name: David's predecessor as king was named Saul. "Paulus" was a well-known surname among the ancient Romans, but is otherwise unknown as a first name. It comes from the Latin word for "short," so it may refer to Paul's size: just call him "Shorty." Interestingly, the name Saul is found only in the Acts of the Apostles, which was written by the author of the Gospel of Luke, and is never found in the letters that Paul himself wrote.

Similar to the naming texts in birth stories already cited, the renaming texts usually give some rationale or explanation for why the individual is acquiring this particular name. For this reason they might be thought of as rebirth texts that describe the creation of a new identity. This is especially so since, as we have seen, they are transitional moments that signal a new status marking the person as no longer the same as he or she was before.

A Brief Biblical Onomasticon

In this final section of the chapter we present a selection of personal and place names found in the Bible with a brief comment on each. It would not be possible to list all the names in the text, so we've chosen these because they are important, interesting, or both. This small sampling gives a taste of what one can learn from, and sometimes the fun one can have with, biblical names.

PEOPLE

Abel – the name of the first murder victim hints that he will be here one day and gone the next because it is the Hebrew term for "vapor, breath" (Gen. 4)

Adam – the name of the first human being is a play on the Hebrew word for "earth" (*'adamah*), from which he was taken

Bathsheba – her name has nothing to do with the bath she is taking when King David first sees her; it means "daughter of abundance," an ironic title for a woman who loses a husband and a child (2 Sam. 11)

David – the "man after God's own heart" has a name that means "beloved"

Eglon – this overweight Moabite ruler has the perfect name ("young calf") for someone who will meet his fate at the business end of a sword wielded by the judge Ehud (Judg. 3)

Judas Iscariot – the name Judas was very common during Jesus' time; there are many theories about the origin of Iscariot, with one proposing that it indicates Judas's hometown and another suggesting that it comes from the Greek word for "assassin"

Mary Magdalene – the second word is not part of her name, but indicates she was from a small town on the Sea of Galilee named Magdala

Michael – the name of this angel is actually asking a question: "Who is like God?" (Rev. 12)

Nabal – the man who unwisely decided to get on King David's bad side was aptly named "fool" (1 Sam. 25)

Pontius Pilate – a comma between the two words would make it clearer; Pilate is his given name, and Pontius identifies the family he comes from

Rachel and Leah – the names of the two sisters Jacob marries mean "ewe" and "cow," respectively; we'll just leave it at that (Gen. 29)

Samson and Delilah – the names of this famous couple give a clue as to how their story will end; a man whose name means "little sun" will have his light extinguished thanks to a woman whose name is similar to the Hebrew word for "night" and might mean "flirt" (Judg. 16)

Zacchaeus – the name of the diminutive man who became a follower of Jesus likely comes from a Semitic root meaning "upright, righteous" (Luke 19)

PLACES

Ai – if you build it they will come; the name of this town destroyed by Joshua and his forces means "the ruin" (Josh. 8)

Armageddon – from the Hebrew words that translate "mount of Megiddo," a city in northern Palestine near major trade routes (Rev. 16)

Babel – humans scattered all across the earth and the different human languages arose when people tried to build a tower in this place that sounds similar to the Hebrew verb "to confuse" (Gen. 11); it also sounds very similar to "Babylon," a place to which many people of Judah were exiled in the sixth century BCE

Eden – take your pick: the name might come from a Hebrew root meaning "fertile, abundant," or it could come from an older Akkadian one that means "plain, steppe" (Gen. 2)

Galilee – this name comes from a Hebrew root that describes roundness, and it likely refers to the shape of the mountains that encircle this northern part of Palestine

Jerusalem – despite the common claim that it means "city of peace," the name more likely is a statement that the city was founded by a pre-biblical god named Shalem

Palestine – derives from the Hebrew term for the Philistines, a people who arrived by sea and settled in the southern coastal area in the twelfth century BCE

Red Sea – the Hebrew words describing this body of water are better translated "Reed Sea"

9 The Real World

Profiting from the Experience

It was featured in Bill Maher's 2008 documentary film *Religulous*, which turned a critical eye toward beliefs and practices associated with organized religion. Timothy Beal devoted a chapter to it in his 2005 book *Roadside Religion*, which recounts his visits to various believe-it-or-not religious attractions throughout America. One recent media story claims that some two thousand people flock to it on a daily basis during the high-tourism season.

We're talking about The Holy Land Experience, a fifteen-acre amusement-park-cum-pilgrimage destination located in the shadow of Disneyworld in Orlando, Florida. The place has been around since 2001 and it's one of the country's best-known Bible-themed vacation spots, an unusual genre of entertainment that has become quite popular.

With many bells and whistles, its website (*www.holyland experience.com*) describes the main attractions at The Holy Land Experience. It boasts the world's largest indoor model of Jerusalem (45 feet by 25 feet), and a separate exhibit that contains a replica of the city's temple. Nearby is a reconstruction of the Qumran caves where the Dead Sea Scrolls were discovered in the mid-twentieth century. The park houses a street market from New Testament times, and the Oasis Palms Café provides welcome respite for the weary. Following Jesus' final footsteps you can make your way along the Via Dolorosa, which ends at Calvary's Garden Tomb. There's even a twice-a-day reenactment of the crucifixion.

We think there are better things to do with thirty-five bucks (20 for kids between 6 and 12 years of age), but judging from the attendance figures not everyone agrees with us. The turnstiles keep spinning at The Holy Land Experience because it gives people something they really crave, and we don't mean close proximity to the Magic Kingdom (although that doesn't hurt). It's nicely summed up in the last word of the name of the place—it provides people the opportunity to have an *experience*, to participate in life as it was lived during biblical times. It's one thing to read about the ancient world. But to see it, walk in it, and, okay, buy a souvenir in it really makes it come alive.

Our purpose is not to criticize The Holy Land Experience and other venues like it. The point is that such places aren't the only resources that can give us a sense of how people lived during biblical times, and usually they're not the most accurate. We can gain much insight about life in the ancient Near East from archaeology and other disciplines, but the Bible remains an excellent jumping-off point. While we can't explore every aspect of the daily life and real world treated in the Bible, we can provide an overview to give some sense of the breadth of what the Bible has to say. Toward that end, we'll discuss some of the buildings and other structures, human activities, food and drink, clothing, and household objects mentioned in the Bible.

Propheting from the Experience

We will begin with the prophetic books, in particular the book of Amos. This is a perfect section of the Bible through which to explore this topic because the prophets were all about daily life and human experiences. This relates to a common misperception about the role the biblical prophets played in their societies. We tend to think of the prophets as predictors and prognosticators who had the ability to peer into the future and tell their contemporaries what was going to happen, like walking and talking horoscopes of the ancient world. Such an understanding misses the point and purpose of prophets in biblical times. They did talk about future events, but their warnings about what was waiting around the corner were always tied to what was happening now right up the street. The prophets didn't make up stuff out of thin air or gaze into a crystal ball and say, "Here's what the future holds." They looked at things around them and said, "In light of what's going on today, here's what will happen tomorrow." In other words, they were concerned with the here and now, the experiences of the present.

Not all versions of the Bible agree on which books are identified as prophetic. The Hebrew Bible of the Jewish community makes a distinction between the Former Prophets and the Latter Prophets, but only the ones in the second group are considered to be prophetic books by Christians. The Former Prophets are comprised of Joshua, Judges, 1 & 2 Samuel, and 1 & 2 Kings—works that are designated as Historical Books by the Christian community. In addition, Christians identify two books as prophetic—Lamentations and Daniel—that Jews do not list among the Latter Prophets. The designation "Historical Books" for Joshua through Kings is due to their content—they present the history of the Israelite people from the time they entered the land until the exile. Lamentations is placed among the prophets by Christians because of its close association with Jeremiah, and there is a long-standing tradition that he was its author. And because Daniel exhibits certain features often linked with prophecy, like the concern with future events mentioned above, it's one of the prophetic books of the Christian canon.

The fifteen books that all groups consider to be prophetic can be divided in a number of ways. Perhaps the most common division is that between the Major Prophets and the Minor Prophets, a distinction based solely on the lengths of the books. By this arrangement Isaiah, Jeremiah, and Ezekiel are the three Major Prophets, and the remaining Minor Prophets are often referred to as the "Book of the Twelve"—Hosea, Joel, Amos, Obadiah, Jonah, Micah, Nahum, Habakkuk, Zephaniah, Haggai, Zechariah, and Malachi.

The earliest prophetic writings in the Bible come from the eighth century BCE, after the land had been divided into a northern kingdom and a southern kingdom. Consequently, it is also common to divide the prophets by geography, with those who directed their messages to Israel referred to as Northern Prophets, and those who spoke to Judah called Southern Prophets. Finally, the time in which it was originally delivered to its audience is sometimes used as a means to designate a prophetic book. The Babylonian Exile, which began in 586 BCE, is the dividing line: the books delivered before that event are described as pre-exilic while those from after it are exilic or post-exilic.

Using these three modes of identifying the prophetic works in the Bible we can label Amos, whose book will be our starting point in the discussion that follows, as an example of a minor, northern, and pre-exilic prophet. He was active in the mid-eighth century BCE during a time when the people in the northern kingdom of Israel were enjoying great prosperity and material success. Well, some of them anyway. A significant gap existed between the haves and the have-nots, and much of Amos's message is an angry denunciation of the way the rich were mistreating and profiting off the poor. Because of its condemnation of this situation, the book of Amos contains some of the Bible's most pointed and powerful comments on social justice.

One final introductory point: prophecy was not something unique or limited to ancient Israel. Prophets were present in neighboring lands throughout the ancient Near East, particularly in Mesopotamia, and many texts have come down to us that describe their roles and contain their utterances. So it's important to keep in mind that Israelite prophecy was just one expression of a wider phenomenon comprised of individuals who claimed authority to interpret and communicate the divine will. We begin each of the following sections with some comments on what Amos has to say about a particular aspect of daily life and then broaden the discussion to consider some of the information provided by other biblical books.

Domiciles

The places in which people lived are mentioned frequently in the Bible. Amos calls attention to the opulent lifestyles of some of the people in the north with his description of their residences in 3:15, where God speaks of the punishment that awaits them. "I will tear down the winter house as well as the summer house; and the houses of ivory will perish, and the great houses shall come to an end." Like well-off people of today who spend the winter in Florida and the rest of the year in northern climes, the upper-class snowbirds of Israel could afford more than one home. Nonetheless, a housing crisis was on the horizon. These abodes might be spacious ("great") and lavishly constructed ("ivory"), but Amos says that they will be destroyed because their occupants have neglected the poor.

Amos makes a similar point in 5:11 when he notes that the well-to-do have constructed homes of hewn stone but they will be denied the pleasure of living in them. A little later in the chapter he calls attention to some of the public spaces of ancient cities when he describes people crying in the squares and wailing in the streets (5:16). There is a likely reference to social stratification in 6:11, where the differences among the classes are reflected in the relative size of their homes: "See, the LORD commands, and the great house shall be shattered to bits, and the little house to pieces."

People did not always live in houses of course, and biblical books set in earlier times sometimes refer to tents. Among the figures who are described as tent-dwellers are Abraham (Gen. 18:1–15), Lot (Gen. 13:5), and Jacob (Gen. 31:33). One of the most graphic murder scenes in the Bible is set in a tent and describes how Sisera, a general in the army fighting the Israelites, flees to Jael's tent only to be killed when she drives a peg through his skull (Judg. 4:17–22). Despite the gruesome nature of the act this brief passage contains references to a number of objects associated with daily life. In addition to the tent and tent peg, we hear about a rug, a skin of milk, and a hammer.

Another story featuring a small living space that offers a rich description of objects from everyday life is 2 Kings 4:10, about a wealthy woman who convinces her husband to take in the prophet Elisha as an occasional houseguest. It is a remarkable verse because it describes the construction of Elisha's quarters and offers an inventory of its furnishings that reads like the ancient equivalent of an IKEA advertisement. "Let us make a small roof chamber with walls, and put there for him a bed, a table, a chair, and a lamp, so that he can stay there whenever he comes to us." By the way, they took on Elisha as a boarder because there were no hotels in ancient Israel. That explains why in some stories, like those in Genesis 19 and Judges 19, local townspeople offer lodging to travelers who are passing through their area.

Also worth noting is the house of Rahab, a prostitute living in Jericho who harbors two spies sent by Joshua to check out the area prior to the Israelites' entry into the promised land (Josh. 2:1–21). This story mentions several intriguing details: the city has a gate that is shut in the evening, Rahab has stacks of flax on her roof that enable her to hide the men, and she helps them escape by letting them down on a rope through her window. Perhaps the most interesting detail is that her house was located on the outer side of the city wall and she lived within the wall itself, a living arrangement observed elsewhere in the biblical world through archeological study.

Speaking of living arrangements, the archeological evidence suggests that the most common domicile in ancient Israel was what is usually referred to as a "four-room house," so named because the space was divided into four sections. These were two-story buildings in which the human occupants lived on the upper level while animals were housed on the ground floor where they could provide warmth and, we imagine, some distinctive household aromas. This helps us understand the story in 1 Samuel 28 when Saul visits a witch at Endor to have her conjure up Samuel's ghost and the text says she had a fatted calf in the house (v. 24).

In the New Testament, houses are sometimes mentioned in Jesus' teachings and miracles. In the parable that concludes the Sermon on the Mount he compares a wise person to one who builds a house on the solid foundation of rock while a foolish person is like someone whose house falls apart because it was built on sand (Matt. 7:24–27). A healing miracle mentioned in all three Synoptic Gospels describes how a group of people remove part of the roof of a house Jesus is teaching in so they can lower down a paralyzed man on a mat. The text is ambiguous, but Mark's version leaves open the possibility that the healing might have taken place in Jesus' own home (2:1–12; cf. Matt. 9:1–8; Luke 5:17–26). Jesus isn't much of a homebody in the rest of the New Testament, but if that's where this story is set we imagine his background in carpentry came in handy after the crowd dispersed. The only clear reference to him at home is found in Matthew's infancy narrative when the Magi enter the house and present the newborn Jesus their gifts of gold, frankincense, and myrrh (2:11). The New Testament also calls attention to the fact that houses sometimes did double duty and served as churches. In the early years of Christianity believers typically gathered together to worship in one of the homes of their members, a practice that is mentioned in several books (1 Cor. 16:19; Col. 4:15; Philem. 2).

Other Buildings

Amos mentions a number of other types of structures in his book, with worship spaces being among the most common. It appears that the people of the north believed their prosperity and good fortune were signs that God was pleased with them, but the prophet challenges this idea. In several passages he voices God's displeasure over their empty rituals and worship services, and calls attention to the places in which these activities occurred.

Two northern towns that contained important shrines were Bethel and Gilgal, and in several passages Amos criticizes the rituals that took place in them. The text of 4:4–5, an indictment God directs toward Israel, drips with sarcasm as it describes what really goes on in these shrines. "Come to Bethel—and transgress; to Gilgal—and multiply transgression; bring your sacrifices every morning, your tithes every three days; bring a thank offering of leavened bread, and proclaim freewill offerings, publish them; for so you love to do, O people of Israel!" (cf. 3:14; 5:5–6; 7:10–13). Elsewhere, the destruction of the north is described as a day in which "the songs of the temple shall become wailings" (8:3). The word translated here as "temple" might also be rendered "palace," so this could be a rare reference in Amos to the royal residence.

The Judean capital of Jerusalem was the location of the main Temple and palace of ancient Judah, and those two buildings are mentioned often in the text. Both were originally built by Solomon, although the Temple was rebuilt when the people returned from exile in the second half of the sixth century BCE, which marked the beginning of what is commonly referred to as the "Second Temple period." It is pointed out that it took Solomon almost twice as long to build the royal palace as it did for him to build the Temple where God would dwell, a comment perhaps meant to call attention to his skewed priorities (1 Kings 6:38–7:1). Some of the most detailed (and mind-numbing) building details in the Bible are found in 1 Kings 6–8 (cf. 2 Chron. 2–4), where the floor plan and furnishings of the temple are described with excruciating precision.

A term commonly used in the Hebrew Bible, especially the Deuteronomistic History, to refer to places where gods other than Yahweh were worshipped is often translated "high places." The precise meaning of the word is debated by scholars, but it likely refers to some type of structure built on a hill or other raised area that housed images of deities or objects associated with them. Perhaps the Bible's best-known reference to a temple dedicated to a god other than Yahweh is the story in Judges 16, in which Samson kills himself and three thousand Philistines who had gathered to offer a sacrifice to their god Dagon by pushing down the columns of the temple and literally bringing down the house.

Residences associated with foreign powers mentioned in the Bible include the palace of the Persian King Ahasuerus, where the beginning of the book of Esther is set (2:8), the palace of the Babylonian King Nebuchadnezzar, who brought Daniel and his friends to serve in his court (Dan. 1), and the headquarters of Pontius Pilate, the Roman official whose jurisdiction included Jerusalem at the time of Jesus' death. The latter's administrative complex is sometimes described using the Latin word *praetorium* (Matt. 27:27; Mark 15:16; John 18:28, 33).

Places of confinement appear throughout the pages of the Bible, indicating that law enforcement and public security were important concerns in antiquity. While he was not literally placed behind bars, the aforementioned Daniel is the Bible's most renowned escape artist. He managed to miraculously survive a den full of lions (Dan. 6:16–28). His three friends—Shadrach, Meshach, and Abednego—similarly survive being thrown into a fiery furnace that was stoked to seven times its usual temperature (Dan. 3:13–30). In both cases, Daniel and his friends emerge unscathed because they remain steadfast in their belief in God. But the title of the Bible's most prominent inmate belongs to Joseph, whose brothers first abandon him in a pit and then sell him off to Egypt, where he was forced to do hard time in jail for a crime he didn't commit when he refused the advances of his boss's wife. His ability to interpret dreams—a skill he shared with Daniel—enables him to get time off for good behavior and to eventually rise to the rank of second-in-command in all of Egypt (Gen. 37; 39–41). Talk about a prison-to-work program.

Each of the four Gospels describes the arrest, torture, and execution of Jesus, who frequently warns that a similar fate awaits those who become his followers. The Acts of the Apostles recounts imprisonment and mistreatment of some of the early Christians, including Peter and John (4:1–22), Peter on his own (12:1–11), and large groups of members of the faith (8:3). It is Paul, though, who is most often persecuted and thrown in jail in Acts (16:19–40; 21:27–36; 28:16), and as the book ends he is living under house arrest in Rome, where according to Christian tradition he was eventually martyred. Scholars are often leery of accepting the historical accuracy of Acts, but Paul's own testimony in letters he wrote confirms that he experienced much hardship that served to validate his role within the community. "Are they ministers of Christ? I am talking like a madman—I am a better one: with far greater labors, far more imprisonments, with countless floggings, and often near death. Five times I have received from the Jews the forty lashes minus one. Three times I was beaten with rods. Once I received a stoning" (2 Cor. 11:23–25a).

A final type of building to be mentioned is the synagogue, a place devoted to Jewish prayer and worship. The origins of the synagogue remain shrouded in mystery. Some have argued that it emerged in Babylon during the exile, while others believe it developed in Egypt in the third century BCE long after the exile. What is certain is that synagogues are not mentioned specifically in the Hebrew Bible. In the New Testament, on the other hand, they are referred to frequently. The Gospels depict Jesus performing miracles (Matt. 4:23; Mark 1:23–27) and teaching (Matt. 13:54; Luke 6:6; John 18:20) in synagogues, and in Luke 4:16–21 he addresses the congregation in a synagogue in his hometown of Nazareth to explain how the prophet Isaiah predicted his coming. The evidence from the New Testament indicates that by the first century CE synagogues were a central and vital part of daily life in Palestine.

Human Activities

The book of Amos contains references to various human activities, some of them productive and others less so. Prophetic works typically do not provide much autobiographical detail, but in 7:14–15 we get a rare reference to a prophet's prior career when Amos mentions that he used to be a herdsman and dresser of sycamore trees who followed the flock. In some passages language related to agriculture and viticulture is used to speak of the relationship between God and Israel in both positive and negative terms. Such imagery is common in biblical literature because society was agrarian-based and the audience could readily understand and relate to the symbolism contained in the texts. "I struck you with blight and mildew; I laid waste your gardens and your vineyards; the locusts devoured your fig trees and your olive trees; yet you did not return to me, says the LORD" (4:9; cf. 4:7). Elsewhere, Amos uses agricultural imagery to paint a more positive picture of the relationship between God and the people (9:13–14).

The negative take on the God-Israel relationship reflects the prophetic view of the mistreatment of the downtrodden by the well-to-do. Experiences from the world of commerce, including business transactions, are drawn upon to show how low some would go to exploit their destitute neighbors. "Hear this, you that trample on the needy, and bring to ruin the poor of the land, saying, 'When will the new moon be over so that we may sell grain; and the sabbath, so that we may offer wheat for sale? We will make the ephah [a unit of measure] small and the shekel [a unit of currency] great, and practice deceit with false balances, buying the poor for silver and the needy for a pair of sandals, and selling the sweepings of the wheat'" (8:4–6).

One verse memorably describes the wealthy women of the fertile region of Bashan living in the lap of luxury while beating down the most vulnerable in society and ordering their husbands about. "Hear this you cows of Bashan who are on Mount Samaria, who oppress the poor, who crush the needy, who say to their husbands, 'Bring something to drink!'" (4:1).

That indictment is repeated and amplified two chapters later in a text that issues a scathing attack on the hedonistic lifestyle of Israel's bluebloods. The scene provides a glimpse into the daily life of Israel's privileged class by describing human activity of a sort that Amos, as a herdsman and dresser of sycamore trees, could not relate to and deplored. "Alas for those who lie on beds of ivory, and lounge on their couches, and eat lambs from the flock, and calves from the stall; who sing idle songs to the sound of the harp, and like David improvise on instruments of music; who drink from bowls, and anoint themselves with the finest oils, but are not grieved over the ruin of Joseph!" (6:4–6). The Hebrew word here that is translated "bowls" refers to a large vessel normally used in worship situations, thus Amos is criticizing the people for both violating sacred rituals by improperly using vessels associated with them and drinking too much.

So why did Amos expect that the upper crust of Israelite society would be able to change its tune and treat the poor with dignity and respect? The answer is found in 5:23–24, which begins with another critical comment about music and ends with one of the book's most celebrated images of social equality. "Take away from me the noise of your songs; I will not listen to the melody of your harps. But let justice roll down like waters, and righteousness like an ever-flowing stream." Some prefer jazz over rock, but God is partial to justice.

In our day and age justice is usually decided in the courtroom, but in the biblical world the city gate was often where justice was meted out. The main entrance to a town was an area buzzing with activity: things were bought and sold, people socialized, and folks came and went. It's the same thing in many parts of the Middle East today. Take the Damascus Gate on the northern side of the Old City of Jerusalem, for example. During certain times of the day it's a sea of people, filled with the hustle and bustle of merchants, customers, and pedestrians. The scene would have been similar in the biblical world, but occasionally the gate would have played the added role of courtroom. This is the background to Amos's comment in 5:10: "They hate the one who reproves in the gate, and they abhor the one who speaks the truth." Amos is criticizing those who don't want to give the poor a fair shake and try to gum up the wheels of justice (cf. 5:12).

The human activities mentioned in Amos are frequently found elsewhere in the Bible, as well as many others he doesn't refer to. Agriculture and viticulture are often discussed, once again highlighting how important the production of food and wine was for society. Similarly, pastoral scenes and the figure of the shepherd are present in many texts. This is undoubtedly one reason why Jesus uses imagery from these settings in his parables and other teachings, including his self-designation as the "good shepherd" (John 10:1–18).

Other outdoor activities referred to in the Bible include hunting and fishing. Amos identifies a common method of hunting when he refers to snares and traps used to catch birds and smaller animals (3:5; cf. Ps. 91:3; Job 18:8–10). In Genesis, Abraham's son Ishmael is described as "an expert with the bow" (21:20), which was the most common way larger animals were hunted and caught. A bit later in Genesis, Esau, the son of Isaac, is also described as a skillful hunter and man of the field. This leads his father to send him off with his bow and arrows in search of game, enabling his twin brother Jacob to trick Isaac and receive the paternal blessing that was rightfully Esau's (Gen. 27).

Fishing and the accoutrements associated with it figure in a number of passages in the Hebrew Bible that mention nets, hooks, harpoons, and spears (Job 41:1–7; Eccles. 9:12; Jer. 16:16; Hab. 1:15). Some of these describe metaphorically the experiences of human beings who are trapped by their enemies, God, or fate. Fishing is an important part of the context and content of many New Testament passages, not least of all because many stories are set on or near the Sea of Galilee and some of Jesus' closest followers were fishermen (Matt. 4:18–22; 13:47–48; 17:24–27; Luke 5:1–11; John 21:4–14).

Since we're sports nuts who subscribe to *Sports Illustrated* rather than *Field and Stream*, we'd be remiss if we didn't take this opportunity to touch on some biblical passages that relate to athletics. Virtually all of them come from the New Testament, which isn't surprising since athletic competition was an important part of the Greco-Roman context in which the Christian writings took shape. Paul clearly knew his way around the gym, a word, by the way, that comes from the Greek word for "naked"; for the Greeks the gymnasium was the place of nakedness. Paul says that becoming a good Christian is like becoming a better athlete, and compares it to the training one undertakes to win a race or a boxing match (1 Cor. 9:24–27; cf. Gal. 2:2; 5:7). Elsewhere the New Testament encourages Christians to train themselves in godliness as they train themselves physically (1 Tim. 4:7–8), to fight the good fight and finish the race so they can win a crown of righteousness similar to those given to champions at athletic events (2 Tim. 4:7–8), and to not run in vain (Phil. 2:16). Such references indicate that even in those pre-ESPN days sports played a vital role in society, but these texts challenge the view that many modern athletics have regarding the connection between sports and religion. Nowhere does Paul or any other New Testament author claim that their success in athletics is due to God being on their side.

Taking Stock

We've seen that, in his critique of the lifestyles of the wealthy citizens of Israel, Amos calls attention to the sumptuous meals and fine wines they enjoy. There are a number of other references to food and drink in his book (2:8; 4:1, 8; 6:4–6; 8:1–2, 13; 9:13–14), as there are in many other places in the Bible. Similarly, Amos and other biblical books often mention clothing and other objects people regularly made use of in their everyday lives (2:6, 8; 8:6). In this closing section of the chapter we'd like to present an inventory of some of the consumables and personal items referred to throughout the text.

Let's start with that most essential of human commodities, food. The promised land is described as "flowing with milk and honey," but there were quite a few other things on the Israelite menu. The following is just a sampling of some of the goodies that people partake of in the Bible: bread, wheat, barley, olives, fig cakes, raisins, curds, pomegranates, apples, salt, dill, cumin, mint, cinnamon, beans, lentils, cheese, and fish (Gen. 18:8; Deut. 14:8–9; 32:14; 1 Sam. 14:24–27; 25:18; 30:12; 2 Sam. 17:29; Job 6:6; Song 4:13–14; Isa. 28:27; Joel 1:12; Matt. 23:23; Mark 9:50; John 21:9–14). That list might sound heavy on the fruits, grains, and legumes, but there was plenty available for the nonvegetarian as well. Animals whose meat could be eaten include ox, sheep, goat, deer, gazelle, roebuck, wild goat, ibex, antelope, and mountain-sheep, in addition to certain fish and clean birds (Deut. 14:4–20). To wash all that down, the most frequently mentioned beverages in the Bible are water, milk, and wine, although many scholars believe beer was also available because of its presence in Mesopotamia and Egypt (Exod. 3:17; 17:1–7; Judg. 4:19; Ps. 104:15; Joel 3:18; John 2:1–11; 4:7–15).

Some of the household items mentioned in the Bible helped to properly prepare and serve all that food and drink. Winepresses and vats were commonly used to make wine (Isa. 16:10; Jer. 48:33; Matt. 21:33), and various jugs, jars, and vessels are mentioned as receptacles for it and other liquids (Gen. 44:1–5; 2 Kings 4:2–6; Mark 9:41; Luke 22:20). Millstones that were used to grind flour in the production of bread are mentioned in a number of places and contexts (Exod. 11:5; Num. 11:8; Judg. 9:53; Isa. 47:2; Matt. 18:6; 24:41; Rev. 18:21). An unnamed woman in Judges 9 turns one into a weapon when she throws an upper millstone from a tower and crushes Abimelech's skull (v. 53).

Among the other household items referred to are baskets (Gen. 40:16–19; Exod. 29:3, 23; Lev. 8:2; Num. 6:15, 17; Deut. 28:5, 17; 2 Kings 10:7; Amos 8:1–2; Mark 6:43), basins (Exod. 30:18–19; John 13:5), and plates and platters (Num. 4:7; Matt. 14:8, 11; 23:25–26). It was all finger food in biblical times, so we don't hear about table settings with forks, knives, and spoons, although a lengthy account of the Temple service does mention forks, along with other food-related objects like cups, plates, bowls, flagons, snuffers, shovels, forks, and basins (Exod. 25:23–30; 27:3). As already noted, larger household furnishings mentioned in the Bible include tables, chairs, lamps, and beds.

Clothing makes its appearance in the very first story in the Bible when Adam and Eve cover up their nakedness by fashioning loin-cloths of fig leaves (Gen. 3:7) and God then upgrades their wardrobe by designing garments of skin for them (3:21). Though frequently mentioned, biblical clothing usually isn't described in any great detail. An exception is the vestments of the priests, which are discussed in painstaking precision down to the most delicate filigree (Exod. 28). Perhaps the most famous article of clothing in the Bible is Joseph's "coat of many colors" that is a symbol of his father's preference for him over his brothers, leading them to sell him into Egypt (Gen. 37). Based on the linguistic evidence, scholars believe that this was not actually a multicolored coat but rather a robe with long sleeves (cf. 2 Sam. 13:18–19).

The way Joseph's clothing functions in his story is a good example of the general principle that physical descriptions in the Bible are usually important to the plot. Each time Joseph's clothing is mentioned it signals a change in his status—the references to his coat indicate he is his father's favorite or he is presumed dead (37:3, 33); the garment he leaves behind with his master's wife lands him in jail (39:13–18); when he changes out of his prison clothes to meet the Pharaoh he becomes free again (41:14); and when Pharaoh dresses him in royal garb he becomes the second most powerful person in Egypt (41:42).

A partial "laundry list" of garments mentioned in the Bible includes the following: sackcloth, usually worn as a sign of mourning (1 Kings 21:27); high-end clothing of superior quality (Ezek. 16:10); loincloth, a type of underwear (Jer. 13:2); sash or waistcloth (Job 12:18); tunic (John 19:23); and purple cloak (Mark 15:17–20). In several stories clothing is used to disguise oneself in order to remain undetected or to deceive another. By disguising themselves Jacob is able to pass for his twin brother Esau (Gen. 27), Tamar tricks her father-in-law Judah into having sexual relations with her (Gen. 38), Saul can visit the female seer at Endor (1 Sam. 28), and the Gibeonites convince Joshua to enter into a treaty with them (Josh. 9). While not the same thing as wearing a disguise, the Bible's only prohibition against cross-dressing might also be noted here (Deut. 22:5).

While accessorizing would not become a fine art until centuries later, the Bible does call attention to jewelry, footwear, and head coverings. The most detailed listing of the baubles and ornaments that were commonly worn is found in Isaiah 3:18–23, an impressive catalog of biblical bling. "In that day the LORD will take away the finery of the anklets, the headbands, and the crescents; the pendants, the bracelets, and the scarfs; the headdresses, the armlets, the sashes, the perfume boxes, and the amulets; the signet rings and the nose rings; the festal robes, the mantles, the cloaks, and the handbags; the garments of gauze, the linen garments, the turbans, and the veils" (cf. Gen. 24:22; 41:42; Exod. 32:2; 35:22; Num. 31:50; Ezek. 16:11–12). Sandals were the footwear of choice in antiquity, as attested in a number of passages (Exod. 3:5; 12:11; Josh. 5:15; Ruth 4:7; Ezek. 24:17; Matt. 10:10; Mark 1:7; Luke 10:4–5; 15:22). As far as head coverings are concerned, there are several references to men's turbans and women's veils (Gen. 24:65; 38:14; Ezek. 24:17), but only the high priest's headdress is described in detail (Exod. 28:40; 29:9). The issue of women covering their heads in church was a concern in early Christianity, and Paul devotes a portion of one of his letters to the matter (1 Cor. 11:4–16).

Bear in mind that the biblical literature was written and took shape over an extended period that covered centuries. Consequently, the details of daily life varied from time to time and from place to place. Our intention in this chapter is not to give the impression that society was static throughout that lengthy period. We've drawn upon literature written across the spectrum of biblical history in order to demonstrate how much one can learn about the world of the Bible from the text itself. Certainly we've barely scratched the surface regarding what life was like in biblical times, and we could have gotten into other things like warfare, transportation, or health care. Much more remains for you to discover on your own, and hopefully what we've covered in this chapter will get you motivated. With no disrespect to the good people behind The Holy Land Experience and places like it, an authentic holy land experience can only be gotten through being familiar with what the Bible and other sources tell us about the ancient world.

There's a Time for Everything

All in the Timing

Ever notice how the Bible tends to pop up and play a prominent role in some of life's key events? Many of these take place in church or other religious contexts, but not all of them. There's always a reading from the Bible when we celebrate becoming a member of a faith community, like at a baptism or a bar mitvah. And even if neither member of the happy couple has set foot in a church since the day *they* were baptized you'll always hear several biblical texts read at church weddings. It's also very common for one of the wedding gifts to be a Bible that will be prominently displayed in the home as a reminder of the vows that were exchanged that day. At death the deceased person's family and friends often recall and celebrate his or her life by reading biblical texts, something that might be done in a church, a synagogue, or at the graveside. In these and other ways, the Bible functions as a marker that calls attention to life's grand events and helps to mark the passage of time.

The same thing happens throughout the year in churches around the world. Roman Catholics and members of many Protestant denominations hear the same readings during religious services every week because they share the same lectionary. (You can find information on the Common Lectionary they all use at *http://www. commontexts.org.*) The lectionary divides the liturgical year into different periods like Advent, Christmas, Lent, and Easter, and assigns readings for each Sunday from the Hebrew Bible and the New Testament. Often the readings have some connection to the particular season, so the Bible becomes a lens through which to reflect upon that time of year's important themes. During much of the year Christians are not preparing for or celebrating big feasts like Easter or Christmas, so the Common Lectionary gives it the wonderfully blasé designation "ordinary time."

But the Bible's presence isn't limited to religious contexts. (Of course, one might object that the very presence of the Bible makes any context religious.) Its role in law courts, where witnesses place a hand on it and swear to "tell the truth, the whole truth, and nothing but the truth" led funnyman George Carlin to dub it "America's favorite national theatrical prop."

Similarly, politicians and other public figures usually have a swearing-in ceremony in which they take the oath of office with one hand on the Good Book. Sometimes that Good Book isn't the one that many people have gotten used to seeing at such moments. Remember the big brouhaha a few years ago when Representative Keith Ellison of Minnesota, the first Muslim elected to the U.S. Congress, opted to take his oath on a copy of the Qur'an?

In these and other ways the Bible is often present during life's Big Moments to add an element of solemnity and weight to the occasion. In other words, the Bible helps to designate and celebrate significant points in the passage of time. In this chapter we're going to flip that around: we'll consider time in the Bible, rather than the Bible in time. Certain days or sets of days are set apart in the Bible for various reasons. Some of them occur frequently and others are extremely rare, so rare that they might not take place in the course of one's lifetime. We explore some of these in this chapter to get a sense of the rhythms and cycles of the biblical notion of time.

Purim: "They Tried to Kill Us—We Won—Let's Eat!"

The late comedian Alan King once remarked that every Jewish holiday can be summed up as follows: "They tried to kill us—We won—Let's eat!" He might have had the book of Esther in mind when he came up with that joke because it encapsulates the basic flow of its plot: the threat of Jewish extinction is followed by vindication, with plenty of food and drink along the way. Esther is set in the Persian

Empire during the reign of a king identified as Ahasuerus. It's a fictional story, but it contains accurate information about Persian culture and society. Most scholars think Ahasuerus is a stand-in for Xerxes I, who ruled Persia between 486 and 465 BCE.

The book recounts the adventures of two Jews living in the Persian capital of Susa, Esther and her cousin Mordecai, who raised her as his own daughter after her parents died. It's an entertaining story full of twists, turns, and reversals of fortune. Like any good tale this one has a hero—a heroine actually—and a villain. The latter role is filled by Haman, Ahasuerus's right-hand man who convinces the king to issue an order calling for the death of all Jews in his kingdom because Mordecai refused to bow down to him. This is where Esther comes to the rescue. When the book opens she is one of many young women in the king's harem, but Ahasuerus becomes smitten by her and she eventually rises to the position of queen. Mordecai convinces her to use her influence to persuade the king to rescind his order to kill all Jews. She is successful in doing so, and the book ends with the establishment of the feast of Purim, commemorating the Jews' victory over their enemies (9:20–10:3).

The exoneration of the Jews is achieved at the expense of Haman, who comes across as a pitiful and laughable character. At one point he believes he is about to be honored by the king for his meritorious service, only to discover that Mordecai is the intended honoree. To add salt to the wound, the king appoints Haman to be in charge of the festivities celebrating Mordecai (6:1–11). A bit later, Haman himself is hanged on the gallows that he had ordered to be built for Mordecai's execution (7:8–10).

Like the account of Joseph in Pharaoh's court (Gen. 37–50), the book of Esther is a story about an Israelite's ability to thrive in a foreign environment that could often be hostile to strangers. It was likely written to encourage Jews in Persia and elsewhere to remain faithful to their beliefs and traditions despite the obstacles they faced. Esther and Mordecai are the ultimate survivors, and they do what they must in order to make their way. This is reflected in their very names: Mordecai and Esther are versions of Marduk and Ishtar, the names of a Babylonian god and goddess, respectively. They take on names associated with local deities in order to fit in, but they never forget their Jewish identity, a factor that is central to the plot. The text subtly reminds us of this by calling attention to Esther's Hebrew name of Hadassah (2:7).

One of the unusual things about the book of Esther is the amount of partying that goes on in it. Ten different feasts are mentioned, and they all entail heavy eating and drinking. The one that begins the book goes on for seven days. "Drinking was by flagons, without restraint; for the king had given orders to all the officials of his palace to do as each one desired" (1:8). Almost one-half of the occurrences of the Hebrew word commonly used for a drinking feast are found in Esther.

Equally unusual is what is not found in Esther. God isn't mentioned a single time in the book, and there are no references to anything religious in the text like prayer, rituals, or the covenant. That lack, and the presence of so much feasting and drinking, helps to explain why there was controversy over including Esther in the Bible. It wasn't fully embraced as part of the Jewish canon until the third century of the Common Era. The Greek version of Esther adds more than one hundred verses to the Hebrew text, and many of these are religious in nature as God has an explicit presence in the story and Mordecai and Esther are more pious by speaking about and outwardly expressing their Jewish faith.

Esther is part of the Writings, the third part of the canon according to the Jewish reckoning. Within that section it is one of a collection of books referred to as the Megillot, or "scrolls," five biblical works that are linked to specific times of the year and read in synagogues on particular feast days. Esther is read each year on the feast of Purim. The other books in the Megillot are Song of Songs (read on Passover), Ruth (Shavuot), Lamentations (Tisha B'Av), and Qohelet (Sukkot).

Purim probably had its origin as a Babylonian or Persian festival, and the book of Esther attempts to explain its legitimacy as a feast of the Jews. It is celebrated on the fourteenth and fifteenth days of the late-winter month of Adar every year as a way of commemorating how Esther and Mordecai helped to deliver the Jews from Haman's plot. The word is the plural form of the Hebrew term *pur*, which means "lot" and refers to the manner by which Haman determined the day to attack the Jews. "In the first month, which is the month of Nisan, in the twelfth year of King Ahasuerus, they cast Pur—which means 'the lot'—before Haman for the day and for the month, and the lot fell on the thirteenth day of the twelfth month, which is the month of Adar" (3:7; cf. 9:24).

Each year the Purim celebration is a festive occasion during which the entire book of Esther is read in the synagogue. Every time Haman's name is mentioned the members of the congregation boo, hiss, and increase the decibel level with noisemakers. A carnival-like atmosphere prevails over the two-day period that includes gifts, costumes, meals, drinking, friends, family—and celebrates the joy of simply being alive. According to the Talmud, an ancient document that is a central source for Judaism, at Purim you should drink until you can't distinguish the difference between the sentences "Cursed be Haman!" and "Blessed be Mordecai!" In some traditions this is accomplished by drinking a shot each time Haman's name is mentioned in the reading of Esther. In any case, Purim is a time to let loose and celebrate. That makes sense, even more so given the story behind this feast: a wily heroine named Esther and her saving of the Jews.

Before we end this section, we want to make clear that we're not advocating binge drinking. As college professors we've seen alcohol contribute to debilitating injuries and even fatalities in the form of both accidents and suicides. We don't endorse the unbridled intoxication that Esther depicts any more than the genocide that it advocates. (Just like we don't endorse quite a few other practices and activities described elsewhere in the Bible.) But Purim is a part of Jewish culture, and the book of Esther that was written for it presents an aspect of the Bible that is often overlooked by modern readers: celebration. This also is one of the moments and one of the dimensions of real life that the Bible describes.

Rest for the Weary

The opening pages of the Bible indicate that even for God there's a time for everything. The first creation story, usually referred to as the Priestly version, presents a very orderly and structured account of how things came to be (Gen. 1:1–2:4a). It's organized like a work week, and each day God creates something new. On the first day light and darkness are created, on the second day the sky is fashioned, and so on through the sixth day when animals and humanity are brought into existence. It's not a rush job, done all at once, but a process that unfolds gradually with each step along the way occurring in its own time.

Anyone who's ever punched a clock knows that the best part of the work week is its end, when you get a chance to unwind, kick back, and recharge the batteries for the next round. And that's precisely what God does after all the heavy lifting of creation. (Actually, the only thing God does in the story is speak, so it was probably the divine vocal chords that were most in need of some R and R.) The text tells us that on the seventh day God took a break: "And on the seventh day God finished the work that he had done, and he rested on the seventh day from all the work that he had done. So God blessed the seventh day and hallowed it, because on it God rested from all the work that he had done in creation" (Gen. 2:2–3).

This passage, like many in the early chapters of Genesis, is an etiology that's meant to explain the origin of something. In this case it provides an explanation for why work is not done on the Sabbath. According to the story the avoidance of labor on that particular day goes back to the beginning of time and is built right into the structure of creation. If God rested on the very first Sabbath, shouldn't we do the same? In fact, the Hebrew verb for "rest" that's used in the verse is very similar to the word for "Sabbath." Scholars debate whether there's an etymological connection between the two, but even if not, the similarity in sound reinforces the point of the passage: the Sabbath is a day of rest.

There was no equivalent to the Sabbath rest in any of Israel's neighboring cultures in the ancient Near East. All indications suggest that the laws and regulations regarding the Sabbath evolved slowly and took a lot longer to take shape than the six days of creation. It might be that the concept of the Sabbath was originally associated with the full moon and only at a later point was it connected to the idea of a day of rest. Whatever its origin, it was certainly a day of rest by the eighth century BCE when the prophet Amos sarcastically mocked the people of his time who were interested only in their next business transaction. "When will the new moon be over so that we may sell grain; and the sabbath, so that we may offer wheat for sale?" (Amos 8:5). By the time of the exile a couple of centuries later Jeremiah was delivering an entire sermon in Jerusalem on the importance of observing the regulation against working on the Sabbath (Jer. 17:19–27; cf. Isa. 58:13–14).

Many people know that Sabbath observance is one of the stipulations of the Decalogue, or Ten Commandments. The command to "keep it holy" is a way of saying that it is a special time of the week that should be devoted to God. What many don't realize is that there are actually two different versions of the Ten Commandments in the Bible, and the biggest difference between them concerns the reason for observing the Sabbath. Exodus 20:8–11 refers directly to the Priestly creation account and says that people should refrain from labor on the Sabbath because God rested on the seventh day after everything had been created. But Deuteronomy 5:12–15 identifies a completely different reason for observing the Sabbath. That passage cites God's bringing the enslaved Israelites out of Egypt as their primary motivation for not working on the Sabbath. As slaves they were forced to work all the time, but now their weekly respite from labor serves as a reminder of the freedom they gained with God's help. This shift reflects one of the main features of the book of Deuteronomy: a special interest in the Exodus as a reason for Israelite beliefs and practices. Some passages say that anyone who violates the Sabbath command should be executed, a punishment that gives new meaning to the expression "working oneself to death" (Exod. 31:12–17; 35:2–3; Num. 15:32–36).

By Jesus' time Sabbath observance was a central element of Jewish life, and the New Testament describes early Christians like Paul going to synagogues on the Sabbath (Acts 13:14; 17:2; 18:4). The Gospels agree that a major source of conflict between Jesus and certain Jewish authorities was his practice of performing healing miracles on the Sabbath, which they considered to be in violation of the law. Eight different Gospel scenes take place on the Sabbath and six of them describe problems between Jesus and Jewish leaders. Most of these involve healing miracles, but not all do (Matt. 12:9–14; Luke 6:6; 13:10–17; John 5:1–18). In Matthew 12:1–8, for example, Jesus is chastised because his disciples pick heads of grain to eat on the Sabbath.

It is sometimes stated that Jesus taught in synagogues on the Sabbath, but the only detailed account of such a scene is found in

Luke's Gospel. It describes Jesus in his hometown of Nazareth, going to the synagogue on the Sabbath "as was his custom," reading from a scroll a portion of the book of Isaiah that speaks of one who has been anointed by God to bring good news to the poor, and claiming that he himself was the fulfillment of that scripture passage (Luke 4:14–30; cf. Mark 1:21–28). There's an interesting reference to a "Sabbath day's journey" in Acts 1:12, which describes the distance one was permitted to travel on a Sabbath according to Jewish law (cf. Matt. 24:20).

These New Testament passages indicate that many of the early Christians were Jews who observed the Sabbath in conformance to the regulations of Judaism. Saturday was therefore an important day of the week for them, but Sunday eventually became the day that was reserved for Christian ritual and worship. This shift was inconsequential to the many Gentiles lacking ties to Judaism who entered the Christian community. But the Sabbath remained an important day for some Christians for a long time, as seen in the fact that it was discussed at church councils as late as the fourth and fifth centuries of the Common Era.

Marking Time

A detailed calendar is not found anywhere in the Bible, but references in the text to annual festivals and information from extrabiblical sources enable us to reconstruct the year with a high degree of confidence. Months were determined by the lunar cycle, and the Bible identifies them in several ways. The most common designation is by number, or order within the year, with the first month occurring in the springtime. This starting point highlights the important role of the agricultural cycle in the structure and annual rhythm of ancient societies (Exod. 23:16; 34:22). In a few passages the months have Canaanite names like Abib (Exod. 13:4; 23:15; 34:18), the first month, and Ziv (1 Kings 6:1, 37), the second month. After the exile the Babylonian names of months were adopted, and seven of these are mentioned in the Hebrew Bible. An example is Adar, the twelfth month of the year, which appears a number of times in the book of Esther (3:7, 13; 8:12; 9:1, 15, 17, 19, 21).

Lists of the main Israelite religious festivals are found in Leviticus 23 and Numbers 28–29. Among the various feasts mentioned there the one most commonly cited in the Bible is Passover, a one-day celebration that centers on the sacrifice of a lamb. Closely associated with it is the Feast of Unleavened Bread, which occurs immediately after Passover and takes place over a seven-day period during which yeast is not used when baking bread. Scholars debate the origins of these two feasts that the Bible sometimes presents as if they are one connected celebration. Passover takes place on the fourteenth day of Nisan, the first month of the year (Lev. 23:5; Num. 28:16), but those who are defiled may celebrate it one month later after being purified (Num. 9:1–14).

A key biblical passage related to Passover is Exodus 12, which explains its origin and is the basis for later celebrations of the feast on into the present day. It's connected to the tenth plague God sent on the Egyptians that resulted in the death of all their first-borns, human and animal, and which made possible the Israelites' Exodus under the leadership of Moses. The text instructs each household to slaughter a lamb and put some of its blood on their doorposts so that God may pass over their homes and not harm their offspring. It also contains specific instructions regarding how they should prepare and eat the meal.

Upon entering the promised land, one of the Israelites' first acts was to celebrate Passover (Josh. 5:10–11). As in Exodus 12, the description of the Passover meal here is immediately followed by a reference to the Feast of Unleavened Bread, underscoring the close connection between the two. According to 2 Kings 23:21–23, after the time of the Judges celebration of Passover was abandoned until it was reinstated by King Josiah as part of his reform effort that was meant to reestablish proper worship in Judah.

Passover is mentioned a few times in the New Testament, with one of the most interesting passages being Luke 2:41–51, the Bible's only "I-thought-the-kid-was-with-you" episode. The text begins by saying that Joseph and Mary used to go to Jerusalem every year to celebrate Passover. When Jesus was 12 years old they returned home without him only to find him several days later in the Temple, wowing the teachers there with his intelligence. It's the only story in the New Testament that describes Jesus as a youth, and is a good reminder to parents always to check and make sure the kid is in the car before you drive off.

In the three Synoptic Gospels, Jesus' Last Supper with his disciples is a Passover meal, and the texts equate it with the Feast of Unleavened Bread even though it technically didn't begin until the day after Passover. "On the first day of Unleavened Bread, when the Passover lamb is sacrificed, his disciples said to him, 'Where do you want us to go and make the preparations for you to eat the Passover'" (Mark 14:12; cf. Matt. 26:17; Luke 22:7). John's chronology is different in that he says that Jesus' Last Supper took place the night before Passover rather than on Passover itself (John 13:1; 18:28; 19:14, 31). There are other interesting differences between John's description of the Last Supper and those of the other Gospel writers: unlike them, he has Jesus wash his disciples' feet, and he does not include Jesus' words about the bread being his body and the wine his blood. John does record a similar saying of Jesus but, curiously, not in the context of the Last Supper (6:48–58).

According to John's chronology, Jesus dies in the hours before Passover begins, and that suits his Christology perfectly. For John, Jesus is the Lamb of God (1:29, 36), and he dies at the very moment when Passover lambs are being slaughtered in preparation for the feast. To ensure the reader makes that connection John is the only writer who provides the detail that Jesus' legs were not broken on the cross because he was already dead. Like the Passover lamb, Jesus is whole and unblemished, and John cites a passage from Exodus about the Passover lamb to reinforce the link. "These things occurred so that the scripture might be fulfilled, 'None of his bones shall be broken'" (John 19:36).

Other Jewish feasts that John mentions are the Festival of Dedication, or Hanukkah (10:22), and the Festival of Booths, or Tabernacles (7:1–14). The former celebrates the rededication of the Jerusalem temple after it was defiled by the Greek ruler Antiochus IV Epiphanes in the second century BCE, and the latter commemorates the Israelites' wandering in the wilderness. As a side note it's worth mentioning that Hanukkah began as a fairly minor holiday in the Jewish calendar that grew in importance many centuries later due to its placement in the year, which put it in competition with Christmas. And, of course, Adam Sandler's *Hanukkah Song* didn't hurt its reputation either (for the electric version see *http://www.youtube. com/watch?v=Vrd9p47MPHg*). The Festival of Weeks, or Pentecost, is referred to in Acts 2. This was a spring barley festival that took place fifty days after Passover and is traditionally recognized in Judaism as the day the law was given to Moses. At the end of Acts there is a reference to "the Fast," generally held to be the Day of Atonement (now known as Yom Kippur), which takes place in the fall and is the most solemn day of the year in Judaism (27:9).

This Land Is Your Land, This Land Is My Land

As college professors there's one aspect of our job that we often get a lot of grief about from our nonacademic relatives and friends: the tradition of the sabbatical. At many colleges and universities every seventh year a faculty member can apply for a year off from teaching, usually at a cut in pay. Contrary to what our jealous acquaintances think, the academic sabbatical isn't meant to be a license to goof off for a year by sitting around eating bonbons, sleeping in, and watching ESPN around the clock (although such abuses have been known to occur). It should be a time of scholarly engagement and productivity that results in some tangible outcome. You are now holding in your hands one such outcome—each of us was on sabbatical for part of the time when this book was being written. So take that, all you brothers-in-law and others who begrudge us because you misunderstand one of the truly great perks of our profession.

Perhaps sabbaticals wouldn't evoke such feelings of resentment if people knew their roots can be traced to the Bible. One context in which we see this is in the command that every seventh year all agricultural land, including vineyards and orchards, should remain unplanted and its produce left ungathered (Exod. 23:10–11). Elsewhere, the Israelites are instructed that every seventh year they are to forgive all debts owed to them (Deut. 15:1–11). Both these regulations functioned as a type of social security meant to allow the poor to help themselves to the fruit of the earth and to be free from the burden of debt. While this is different from the point behind an academic sabbatical the connection between the two should be apparent: the seventh year is a time to shift gears and not act the way you did in the previous six.

The idea of a sabbatical year is further developed in the Bible through the introduction of the jubilee year, both of which are treated in detail in Leviticus 25. The name *jubilee* comes from the Hebrew word for a ram, and the text states that a trumpet, or ram's horn, was to be blown to signal the commencement of the jubilee year (Lev. 25:9). The jubilee year took place every fifty years after seven cycles of seven sabbatical years, and its primary purpose was to maintain equitable distribution of property. Land that had been sold reverted back to its original owners, debts were forgiven (vv. 35–37), and Israelites who had sold themselves into slavery were free to return to their own land and households (vv. 39–46).

The jubilee year might be related to the practice attested in the ancient Near East of granting amnesty or release to citizens at the beginning of the reign of a new king. With that model in mind God is the king, and there is a theological dimension to the jubilee year in addition to its sociological purpose of meeting the needs of the economically disadvantaged. Regardless of who might own it at a given moment, all land ultimately belongs to God, the supreme land-lord, who is free to give it to anyone. "The land shall not be sold in perpetuity, for the land is mine; with me you are but aliens and tenants" (Lev. 25:23).

Isaiah 61:2 mentions an individual who proclaims a year of favor from the Lord that sounds very similar to the jubilee year because of its focus on freedom and equity. "The spirit of the LORD God is upon me, because the LORD has anointed me; he has sent me to bring good news to the oppressed, to bind up the brokenhearted, to proclaim liberty to the captives, and release to the prisoners; to proclaim the year of the LORD's favor, and the day of vengeance of our God; to comfort all who mourn" (Isa. 61:1–2). This is an important text in the New Testament also because, as we saw earlier, Luke describes Jesus reading it in the synagogue at Nazareth and then claiming that he is the fulfillment of Isaiah's prophecy (Luke 4:14–21). Despite the indignant response of his neighbors to that claim, the spirit of compassion and concern for the poor that is behind the jubilee year is very much at the heart of the message Jesus preached.

There is no record of the jubilee year ever being enacted in Israel's history, and therefore many scholars believe it is an idealistic vision that was never practically applied. Despite its absence from the historical record, we're glad it and the sabbatical year are on the books. Otherwise, we'd be like every other working stiff.

That'll Be the Day

Earlier in this chapter we discussed how time functions in the creation account, so we think it fitting that we conclude it with a brief discussion of the other end of the continuum. What does the Bible say about the end of time? This is a topic that is of special importance to the prophets of the Hebrew Bible and is also addressed by a number of New Testament writers. Various designations containing the word *day* are used in the Bible to refer to the end time, with a common one being "the day of Yahweh" or "the day of the LORD."

We're not exactly sure who came up with the term "the day of LORD," but by the eighth century BCE it was already in use as seen in the book of Amos. "Is not the day of the LORD darkness, not light, and gloom with no brightness in it?" (Amos 5:20; cf. 5:18). The day of the Lord will be a time of reckoning and judgment. Most passages that refer to it, as here, strike an ominous note and issue a clear warning about it. Other texts, though, offer a word of comfort because the day of the Lord is when Israel's enemies will be held accountable and punished. This is typically the message in the oracles against the nations, which are commonly found in the prophetic books. At the beginning of an oracle against Babylon, for example, Isaiah says, "Wail, for the day of the LORD is near; it will come like destruction from the Almighty!" (Isa. 13:6–8; cf. Isa. 13:9–22; Jer. 46:10–12; Ezek. 30:1–9). That's definitely good news for the people of Judah.

But sometimes Israel or Judah is on the receiving end of an oracle of judgment and the day of the Lord spells doom for the chosen people. This is a central theme of the book of Zephaniah, which refers to the day of the Lord to speak of a global destruction that will not spare Judah. "The great day of the LORD is near, near and hastening fast; the sound of the day of the LORD is bitter, the warrior cries aloud there. That day will be a day of wrath, a day of distress and anguish, a day of ruin and devastation, a day of darkness and gloom, a day of clouds and thick darkness" (Zeph. 1:14–15; cf. 1:7–13, 18; 2:1; 3:8, 11).

Related expressions like "the day," "that day," and "day of vengeance" occur nearly two hundred times in the Bible to describe the end time, and some of them refer to a period of woe and punishment while other texts speak of reward and plenty (Isa. 2:2–4; 11:10; 19:18–25). Among the things people will enjoy are good health and prosperity (Isa. 29:18–19; 30:26), ample food and drink (Isa. 4:2; 7:21–22; 25:6–9; 30:23–24), and peaceful coexistence (Isa. 11:1–10; Hos. 2:18).

In the New Testament, the day of the Lord and related terms refer to Jesus' return at the end of time. In the Gospels it is commonly designated as "the day" or "that day" (Matt. 7:22; 25: 13; Mark 14:25; Luke 17:22–31; 21:34; John 14:18–20; 16:22–23, 26; cf. Acts 2:20; 1 Cor. 1:8). Many passages warn about the need to be prepared for the end time because it will arrive unexpectedly (2 Pet. 3:10). Early in his career Paul believed that Jesus' return was imminent, and this was why he thought it was unnecessary for Christians to marry (1 Cor. 7:8). If the end of the world is around the corner, what's the point of procreating? "For this we declare to you by the word of the Lord, that we who are alive, who are left until the coming of the Lord, will by no means precede those who have died" (1 Thess. 4:15; cf. 2:19; 3:13; 5:23).

Unfortunately, our examination of some of the main aspects of the biblical understanding of time has itself "run out of time." But one thing you should have learned in reading this chapter is that the Bible's notion of time is a predominantly cyclical one. If you missed something this time around, no worries—it'll be back when the time is right again. Events and celebrations recur with regularity and predictability, whether it's the weekly Sabbath, the annual Purim feasting and drinking, or the twice-a-century jubilee year. Like a carousel, the cycle of life goes round and round, and the Bible provides a road map for the never-ending journey.

"In This Corner...": Competing Perspectives

Who Says?

If you're a student in one of our courses and you want to make our eyes bulge while we turn several shades of purple, all you have to do is utter three simple words: "the Bible says." Like most of our Bible scholar colleagues, nothing gets our dander up quite like that seemingly innocuous phrase followed by whatever the person speaking it chooses to insert. We're on a mission to expunge it from our students' vocabularies, but we know we're probably fighting a losing battle because the enemy is everywhere. A quick Google search of the words "the Bible says" shows that they are found almost 17 million times in cyberspace. That's nowhere near as common as those other three little words—"I love you" pops up more than 90 million times—but it's still a very impressive showing. (We're not sure what to make of this, but a search for the words "the Bible says I love you" produces only four measly hits.)

Why do we get so annoyed when someone tells us what the Bible says, or "sez" (that alternate spelling yields more than 60,000 Google hits)? For one thing, the Bible doesn't *say* anything in the literal sense of the word. It's a written text, and as such it must be read and interpreted to have any meaning. Interpretation is a human activity that is shaped by a reader's context and personal background, and so different people will understand the same text differently. Therefore a text does not say or mean only one thing, but is capable of a variety of meanings that are all generated by flesh-and-blood readers engaged in the act of interpretation. So it would be more accurate to say "here's what the Bible means to me" rather than "here's what the Bible says."

Another reason why we hyperventilate when people put words in the Bible's imaginary mouth is that they fail to recognize the highly complex nature of the biblical material. The Bible looks, feels, and smells like a book, but it isn't just *a* book. Sure, it has two covers and its pages are numbered sequentially, but it's actually a collection of books. Our point is that each individual composition has its own history of development and transmission. In fact, many biblical books are themselves comprised of separate and distinct parts that were originally independent until they were eventually compiled and brought together by an editor. To hold the Bible is to have a mini-library in one's hand. It's the ancient equivalent of a Kindle.

The person who claims to know what "the Bible says" assumes the text speaks with one voice and ignores the incredible diversity of perspectives within it. It's a diversity that we're constantly bumping up against in the modern world. We defy you to name a major social issue of our time that hasn't been discussed in light of the Bible. Poverty, war, racism, gender, capital punishment, homosexuality, abortion, the environment—you name it, in each case the Bible has been brought into the conversation. Sometimes it seems like politicians turn to the Good Book more than preachers do.

The really fascinating thing is that the Bible is regularly cited to support or justify various positions on each of those issues. Whether you're pro or con, for or against, the Bible can usually be appealed to if you want to defend your view. To cite just one example, let's take God's command to humanity in Genesis 1:28 to exercise dominion over the earth. Some take it as permission for humans to control and dominate other living creatures and the natural world, while others see the very same verse as a charge for us to be stewards who must act responsibly and in harmony with the rest of creation.

That's the interpretive process at work. One person's "Avoid the spill!" is another's "Drill, baby, drill!" Such a range of views is possible because the Bible contains an amazing array of perspectives on various matters, a topic we will explore in this chapter. Sometimes it offers contradictory messages on big questions like the meaning of human existence and how life should be lived. Elsewhere it presents different versions of the same events that are hard to reconcile. In some cases biblical figures appear to have split personalities as they say or do something in one book that the authors of another book couldn't imagine them doing. The presence of these conflicting perspectives is a caution against making generalizations about the Bible's contents and a reminder to avoid the three words that shall not be spoken.

The Wise Guys

An excellent way to get a sense of how the Bible can send mixed messages is to compare the books of Job and Qohelet (also known as Ecclesiastes). Both works wrestle with questions related to the meaning of life and the human condition, but they don't see eye-to-eye on what it all means or humanity's place in the larger scheme of things. Along with the book of Proverbs, Qohelet and Job comprise a section of the Hebrew Bible that is commonly referred to as the "Wisdom writings." Other portions of the text, like certain psalms, also contain features associated with Wisdom literature, but these three are the only books given that designation.

Wisdom literature is not unique to the Bible. There are many examples of it from other areas of the ancient Near East like Egypt and Mesopotamia, and it is also found in many cultures in other parts of the world. The reason for its widespread presence is that Wisdom literature addresses perennial concerns that are basic to all human beings and that transcend the differences among us. It does this not by bombarding readers with facts or persuading them with erudite disquisitions that employ flawless logic. Instead, Wisdom literature appeals to common human experience to make its case and probe the complexities of life. An effective piece of Wisdom writing leaves the reader thinking, "Yeah, I can relate to that," rather than "Wow, I never thought of that."

This underscores the difference between wisdom and intelligence. Intelligence is typically associated with the accumulation of knowledge through formal education, book learning, and similar means. But wisdom is attained in other ways, most commonly through experience and just plain living. It's like street smarts and common sense: they can't teach you that stuff in school. The longer you live and continue to learn from your experiences, the wiser you can become. That's undoubtedly why wisdom is often associated with the elderly. When was the last time you saw a young person play a sage on a television show or in a movie?

The distinction between wisdom and intelligence is most apparent when really smart people do really dumb things. We all know very bright folks who aren't particularly wise, and vice versa. Our line of work is full of brainiacs, but sometimes all that gray matter can cover up a serious lack in the wisdom department. We'll spare you the details, mainly to avoid a lawsuit, but our experiences in academia tell us it isn't uncommon for someone with a lot of letters after his or her name to go off the rails and down in flames for acting unwisely. One of the aims of Wisdom literature, like the books of Qohelet and Job, is to instruct people about the ways of the world and therefore lessen the likelihood of a disastrous outcome.

The book of Qohelet contains the observations, musings, and reflections of a man who has thought long and hard about the meaning and purpose of life. It's one of the latest of the books of the Hebrew Bible, probably composed sometime around 250 BCE in a Hellenistic Greek context. In many places, the book's message is at odds with the prevailing attitudes found elsewhere in the Hebrew Bible, a difference likely due in part to its late date, which put its author in contact with Greek philosophical thought.

Qohelet's basic view of life is nicely summarized in the second verse of his book, which is then repeated almost verbatim at the end of the work. "Vanity of vanities, says the Teacher (Heb. *qohelet*), vanity of vanities! All is vanity" (1:2; cf. 12:8). This organizational principle, by which a key word or phrase is repeated at the beginning and end of a composition, is called an *inclusio*. It usually draws the reader's attention to a central theme of the work. In this case, the Hebrew word translated "vanity" is *hebel*, a term that can mean "vapor, breath" and refers to something that is fleeting or transitory in nature. It is found more than thirty times in Qohelet, and so it runs like a thread throughout the entire book as a reminder of the emptiness and futility of life.

According to Qohelet, human existence is absurd and nothing but a random series of meaningless events. He says that's the way things have always been and it's the way they always will be, so there's no point in trying to change things. "What has been is what will be, and what has been done is what will be done; there is nothing new under the sun" (1:9). The worst thing about this situation is that it's so unfair. There is no system of reward and punishment, so all people, whether good or bad, share the same fate and end up in eternal oblivion. "For there is no enduring remembrance of the wise or of fools, seeing that in the days to come all will have been long forgotten. How can the wise die just like fools?" (2:16). While not quite suicidal, Qohelet prefers nonexistence to the shallow and empty life he knows. "And I thought the dead, who have already died, more fortunate than the living, who are still alive; but better than both is the one who has not yet been, and has not seen the evil deeds that are done under the sun" (4:2–3).

Qohelet thinks all we can do is accept this miserable state of affairs and try to enjoy life as much as possible. The call to eat, drink, and be merry is found throughout the book and functions as a refrain that advises people on how to live. "This is what I have seen to be good: it is fitting to eat and drink and find enjoyment in all the toil with which one toils under the sun the few days of the life God gives us; for this is our lot" (5:18; cf. 2:24; 3:13; 8:15; 9:7; 10:19). As this quote indicates, Qohelet believes it is impossible for humans to know the divine will. God's ways are inscrutable and unknowable, and so the only proper response is to have fear and awe of God, another theme the author repeats frequently in the book. "I know that whatever God does endures forever; nothing can be added to it, nor anything taken from it; God has done this, so that all should stand in awe before him" (3:14; cf. 5:7; 7:18; 12:13).

Most people have had exposure to Qohelet's thought and ideas without ever being aware of it. The folk musician Pete Seeger adapted the words of the poem in 3:1–8 for his song *Turn, Turn, Turn*, which became a huge hit for the rock group The Byrds in the 1960s and continues to enjoy much airtime on the radio. The chapter's opening three verses capture the tone and message of the entire piece. "For everything there is a season, and a time for every matter under heaven: a time to be born, and a time to die; a time to plant, and a time to pluck up what is planted; a time to kill, and a time to heal; a time to break down, and a time to build up" (3:1–3). The predictability and cyclical nature of life is to the fore in this passage, which claims there is a logic to the world that is ultimately beyond our grasp. Qohelet says as much a few verses later when he acknowledges the gap that will always exist between God and humanity. "He has made everything suitable for its time; moreover he has put a sense of past and future into their minds, yet they cannot find out what God has done from the beginning to the end" (3:11).

So how did such a pessimistic and depressing book end up in the Bible, especially since it disagrees so strongly with what's said elsewhere in the biblical writings? For one thing, its presumed association with King Solomon didn't hurt. Although Solomon isn't mentioned by name anywhere in it, the opening words of the book refer to the author as "the son of David," and elsewhere he describes himself as the king of Israel (1:12). Although the book comes from long after Solomon's time and critical biblical scholarship does not consider him to be its author, the book's loose connection with him likely played a role in Qohelet being accepted into the biblical canon.

Affixed to the book's end is an epilogue that was not written by Qohelet's original author but that probably also played a role in its acceptance. The final two verses of Qohelet contradict much of what has been said in the previous twelve chapters by claiming that people will be judged based on whether or not they follow the law of God. This effectively turns the book's central message on its head and introduces the notion that there is a degree of justice and rationality to the world and human existence. In a sense, we have here a competing perspective within a book that itself offers a competing perspective to the received common wisdom reflected in the other biblical literature. As relatively brief as this two-verse section might be, it may have rehabilitated the book in the eyes of those responsible for including it in the canon. "The end of the matter; all has been heard. Fear God, and keep his commandments; for that is the whole duty of everyone. For God will bring every deed into judgment, including every secret thing, whether good or evil" (12:13–14). The book's original author likely would have read that and said, "Huh?"

Yet another reason why Qohelet might have received the seal of approval is because there's a certain element of truth to its message. Let's face it—who among us doesn't occasionally wake up on the wrong side of the bed or question the point of it all? It comes with our skin. Sometimes life seems like the proverbial riddle wrapped around an enigma, and the most natural response is to scratch our head and ask for a do-over. That sentiment isn't expressed anywhere else in the biblical literature, and yet it's a fundamental experience that we all have. You might say giving it a voice in the Bible was a very wise decision.

Job is a much longer Wisdom book that can be paired with Qohelet because it too is concerned with life's Big Questions, in this case primarily the issue of why innocent people suffer. It's a difficult work to date but most scholars place it in the sixth century BCE during the exile, a turbulent time when many of the traditional views and ways of looking at the world were being called into question.

Unlike Qohelet, the book of Job teaches that there is logic and order to life, an idea best seen in the notion that good people are rewarded and sinners are punished. Job would never accept Qohelet's advice to passively accept his lot in life, kick back, and pop open a cold one. He prefers a more aggressive approach and challenges God head-on. There is a clue to this aspect of his personality in his name, Job, which means something like "Where is the father (God)?" This is a guy who's looking for answers and will go right to the top to try to get them.

The book of Job comprises three parts and might be thought of as a "poetry sandwich." A prologue (1:1–2:13) and an epilogue (42:7–17), both written in prose, surround a poetic core in 3:1–42:6. The prose sections, which seem to have been originally one composition until it was split into two parts so that the poetry could be inserted between them, are probably the older portion of the book. They tell the story of a righteous man who loses all his possessions but remains faithful to God and eventually receives everything back. God even restores the children Job lost by replacing them with new ones. Most of the poetry is found in a series of three cycles of speeches (the third one is incomplete) in which Job has a conversation with three friends about the reasons behind his misfortune, and a fifth figure also weighs in on the topic (chs. 32–37). The dramatic high-point of the poetry is found in chapters 38–41 when, in a lengthy speech, God responds to Job's demands to be heard.

In the poetry Job's friends often espouse a cause/effect view of things and maintain that he must have done something to deserve the misery he is experiencing. At one point one of them tells him, "Does God pervert justice? Or does the Almighty pervert the right? If your children sinned against him, he delivered them into the power of their transgression. If you will seek God and make supplication to the Almighty, if you are pure and upright, surely then he will rouse himself for you and restore to you your rightful place" (8:3–6; cf. 4:7–9; 18:5–21; 20:1–11). Similarly, Job often asserts his innocence and insists he has done nothing wrong, and so he appears to buy into the idea that God rewards the just and punishes only the guilty. "Though I am innocent I cannot answer him; I must appeal for mercy to my accuser" (9:15; cf. 1:22; 2:10; 9:20–21; 10:14; 13:23; 27:6). In this way, the characters express a belief in a certain order and justice in the world that is lacking in most of Qohelet.

This results in two different views of God for Qohelet and Job. Qohelet's deity is inaccessible and beyond the reach of human comprehension. As people fumble their way blindly through the absurdity that is human existence they can only accept the hand God has dealt them. For Qohelet, God remains a mystery to be pondered and is the root of the problem that is at the heart of life. Job, on the other hand, believes that God is the solution to the problem. He knows himself to be innocent and so he wants his day in court to make his case to God. Throughout the book he rails against God, and in several places Job calls God out and demands a hearing to settle the matter once and for all. "I would lay my case before him, and fill my mouth with arguments. I would learn what he would answer me, and understand what he would say to me. Would he contend with me in the greatness of his power? No; but he would give heed to me. There an upright person could reason with him, and I should be acquitted forever by my judge" (23:4–7; cf. 10:2; 13:3, 18–19). There is a relational dimension to Job's understanding of God that Qohelet does not possess. Qohelet is content to talk *about* God, but Job demands to talk *to* God.

And God takes the bait. The divine speech in chapters 38–41 is an impressive *tour de force* in which God turns the tables on Job. In a scene that resembles a weird parody of *Jeopardy!* God answers Job's questions with more questions. God bombards Job with almost sixty questions in these four chapters, and virtually all of the rest of the time God is either setting up or commenting on those questions.

For the most part they're rhetorical questions meant to put Job in his place. The opening one sets the tone for what follows. "Who is this that darkens counsel by words without knowledge?" (38:2). In other words, "Job, you don't know diddly-squat!" This leads to a series of queries to which Job can only reply, "No," "Of course not," "You've got me there," or something similar. The first of the series is a well-placed blow with a touch of sarcasm that's meant to take the wind out of Job's sails. "Where were you when I laid the foundation of the earth?" (38:4). Ouch.

God piles it on a bit, but at least they had the chat. Through this exchange Job comes to realize that God's ways are not his ways and that he has no business questioning God's motives or methods. Now you might say that that's exactly the conclusion that Qohelet has reached, without the bruised ego. True enough, but they each arrive at that point in a different way, and therein is found the key difference.

Qohelet doesn't have a conversation with God, and he'd probably consider it to be a waste of time. For him, God is disinterested and distant. Job, though, doesn't think of God as some aloof, mysterious presence, but as a dialogue partner who responds to human needs and requests. Neither has clue one about God's ways, but Job knows something Qohelet doesn't: God hears and pays attention. This shows that biblical wisdom doesn't come in a one-size-fits-all package, but rather takes different forms and shapes. To claim "the Bible says" this or that about wisdom or the divine-human relationship is to misinterpret the evidence.

Two Pairs of Kings

Another good example of competing visions in the Hebrew Bible can be seen in the differences between the Deuteronomistic History (DH) and the Chronicler's History (CH). The DH presents a highly theologized account of the history of the Israelite people that runs from the book of Joshua through 2 Kings. It covers the period from the wandering in the wilderness after the Exodus up until the Babylonian Exile in 586 BCE. The CH, found in 1 and 2 Chronicles, has its own theological agenda but is more limited in scope, covering only the period of the United Monarchy under David and Solomon and the subsequent history of the kingdom of Judah.

In their portrayals of David and Solomon the DH and CH share much in common, but they diverge in some important ways. It's pretty clear that the CH, which appears to have been written much later, has used the DH as its main source, but it adds its own spin to the description of the time of the United Monarchy. In particular, it omits material that doesn't fit its agenda: virtually all of the passages that view David and Solomon negatively are left out in its retelling of their reigns. A similar thing often occurs in American politics when Republicans and Democrats offer wildly different versions of the accomplishments and failings of a particular administration depending on its president's party affiliation.

In this case, whoever is responsible for the CH is a member of the "David/Solomon party." Their reigns are described in 1 Chronicles 10 to 2 Chronicles 9, a section that covers twenty-nine chapters, and this period is presented as the Golden Age of Israel. We don't have time to identify all the ways the CH buffs David's and Solomon's images and removes the chinks from their armor, so a few examples will have to suffice. Perhaps the sleaziest episode in David's (or any other biblical character's) life is described in the DH in 2 Samuel 11–12. Those chapters explain how he has sexual relations with a woman named Bathsheba and then is forced to have her husband killed to hide the fact that he is the father of the child she now bears, a child who dies soon after birth as punishment from God. To save his own reputation, David is forced to lie, cheat, manipulate, and abuse his power in ways that would make any slimeball with an ounce of decency blush. This story is completely missing from the CH, which goes to great lengths to present David as an honest and upright person who is beyond reproach.

The CH also portrays David as a pious, God-fearing man who is the founder of Israel's cultic system. This is seen most clearly in his relationship to the Temple. In the DH, David expresses his desire to build a house for God. But once the prophet Nathan informs him that this is a task that will fall to his son (2 Sam. 7), David has no further involvement or interest in the Temple. In the CH, on the other hand, David plays a significant role in the building of God's house as he provides the personnel, provisions, and even the blue-print to facilitate its construction.

Solomon's reputation is also scrubbed clean in the CH, which presents him as an unblemished chip off the old block. His ascent to the throne in the DH is described in 1 Kings 1–2, a section that raises some questions about the legitimacy of his succession. It describes a frail, dying David being manipulated by Nathan and Bathsheba to put Solomon on the throne as his older brother Adonijah stakes his claim to it. Before David expires he manages to rally a bit as he and the newly crowned Solomon have their last father-and-son talk. During that conversation David tells him, in a series of "wink-wink, nudge-nudge" comments, to bump off the enemies that might pose a threat, and then he gives up the ghost. Not surprisingly, none of this material made its way into the CH because it would raise eyebrows regarding David's character and Solomon's legitimacy. The same is true of 1 Kings 11, where the DH lists all the sins and offenses of Solomon that led to the end of the United Monarchy and its division into the northern and southern kingdoms.

Some great descriptions of palace intrigue and the Bible's best deathbed scene are lost on the cutting-room floor in the CH's sani-tized version of the reigns of David and Solomon. The outcome is that the two kings emerge with their reputations untarnished, and they can be put forward as the quintessential great rulers who were rewarded by God for their virtuous ways. But when we place the DH and CH versions side-by-side it's obvious that more than one David and Solomon haunt the pages of the Bible, and their double lives raise some provocative and intriguing questions.

Who Do People Say He Is?

Perhaps the best place in the New Testament to get a proper sense of the multi-voiced nature of the Bible is the Gospel material. The so-called Synoptic Gospels—Matthew, Mark, and Luke—are similar in many ways but they also diverge and disagree often, with each containing stories not found in the others and presenting its own understanding of who Jesus was. But things really get interesting when we compare the first three Gospels with John, who presents a portrait of Jesus that is at times barely recognizable in light of what the Synoptics say about him. It's like being on an elevator and hearing a Muzak version of one of your favorite songs: it's somehow similar to the original version and yet worlds apart.

People often talk about the Gospels as if all four agree on what Jesus said and did, but that's clearly not the case. Some of the best-known features of the gospel genre never appear in John's account. For example, he doesn't have Jesus speak a single parable, and yet that distinctive style of Jesus' teaching pops up all over the place in the other three Gospels. Similarly, John's Jesus rarely mentions the kingdom of God and never mentions the kingdom of heaven, although these expressions are central to Matthew, Mark, and Luke. While the Synoptic Gospels each record numerous miracles performed by Jesus throughout the course of his ministry, John has only seven (a highly symbolic number in the Bible), all found in the first half of his Gospel.

The four Gospels have very few scenes in common, and even where they do John spices things up with some surprising twists and turns. For instance, all four report that just before his death Jesus had a "Last Supper" with his closest followers. According to the Synoptics, at this meal Jesus refers to the bread and wine they partake of as his body and blood, and this became the basis for one of the most important rituals in Christianity. True to form, John goes in a completely different direction. His account of the Last Supper makes no reference to the bread or wine, but it includes a description of Jesus washing the feet of his disciples, a scene that is itself reenacted in countless churches around the world on the Thursday before Easter.

On the flip side, there are many scenes, people, and elements in John that have no counterparts in Matthew, Mark, or Luke. For example, only in John's Gospel does Jesus change water into wine at the wedding feast in Cana (2:1–11), have an extended conversation with a Samaritan woman at a well (4:1–42), and heal a man blind from birth (9:1–41). The Fourth Gospel is also the only one to make reference to an enigmatic figure known as Jesus' "beloved disciple" (13:23; 19:26; 20:2; 21:7, 20).

In his teachings John's Jesus constantly refers to himself, something he rarely does in the other three accounts of his life. In John he uses the "I am" formula an astounding forty-six times, and he identifies himself in some curious ways at times. Among others, Jesus is the light of the world (8:12), the bread of life (6:35), the resurrection and the life (11:25), the gate (10:7), the good shepherd (10:11), and the true vine (15:1). Meanwhile, the Jesus of the Synoptics never uses any of these descriptors to refer to himself. John probably makes use of this technique so frequently because he wishes to equate Jesus with God, who introduces himself to Moses as "I am" (Exod. 3:14).

Maybe Jesus' defining trait in John's Gospel is that he is in complete control of things at all times. This is seen most vividly in the passion narrative, the last part of each of the four Gospels that describes Jesus' death and the events leading up to it. When John recounts Jesus' arrest in the garden of Gethsemane, Jesus is not praying that he be released from what awaits him as he does in the other three Gospels. In fact, John states explicitly that Jesus is aware of everything that is about to happen to him (18:1–4). On his way to the cross and certain death, John's Jesus carries his own cross (19:16–17), unlike the Jesus in the Synoptic Gospels, who is assisted by another man. When Jesus takes a drink while he is on the cross, John remarks that he does so not because he is thirsty but because he has to fulfill the scriptures (19:28). Jesus' final words in John are not "My God, my God, why have you forsaken me?" as in Matthew and Mark, or "Father, into your hands I commend my spirit," as Luke has it. John's Jesus utters a confident "It is finished" as he expires, sounding every bit like someone who has accomplished what he or she set out to do (19:30). Even John's description of Jesus' death contains a subtle reference to Jesus being in control until the very end. The Synoptic Gospels state that Jesus "breathed his last," but John says that he "bowed his head and gave up his spirit." In the Fourth Gospel Jesus' life isn't taken from him, he hands it over (19:30).

All these differences, and many others that could be added to them, are due to the contrasting Christologies found in Matthew, Mark, Luke, and John. We don't have just one portrait of Jesus in the Gospels, but four. And if we add the writings of Paul and the other New Testament authors into the mix, the number of competing Jesus portraits present in the New Testament grows accordingly. So the answer to the question that began this section ("Who do people say he is?") is, "It depends on what you read."

Some people are troubled or threatened by the presence of competing views and perspectives in the Bible. They believe that if the Bible doesn't speak with one clear voice on everything it somehow diminishes the sacred nature of the text or calls into question its status as God's word. The beliefs of such people should always be respected, but to have this attitude is to miss out on some very important dimensions of the biblical literature. As we noted at the outset of this chapter, the Bible is a diverse set of writings that developed and took shape over a long period of time. Each one of them emerged within and responded to a particular set of circumstances far removed from our own. When the same topic or material was being discussed it was natural and unavoidable that it would be treated differently depending on the time and place in which the writing was being developed, and the immediate audience for whom it was written. How could it be otherwise? Ironically, what might appear to be a threat is actually a marvelous opportunity. Job and Ecclesiastes, the DH and the CH, and the four Gospels all coexist within the same Bible, and that gives us an opportunity that their original audiences most likely never had. We get to listen to, reflect upon, and learn from them and the many other voices that emerge from the Bible.

All You Need Is Love

What's Love Got to Do with It?

The Bible, that is. If you were to conduct a survey and ask people how the Bible treats the topic of love, most would probably respond by drawing on a number of stock themes or passages that are well-known to anyone possessing even a passing familiarity with the biblical tradition. They would undoubtedly refer to things like the love of God, loving your neighbor as yourself, and loving your enemy. And they would be correct because these are important teachings found in the biblical text that are meant to guide people in their daily lives.

But these things don't encompass everything the Bible has to say on the subject. Love of one's neighbor and enemy are concepts meant to influence our views and attitudes toward others, and they can be helpful in shaping our mind-set. But they're abstract theoretical principles that don't address the tangible aspects of love, the nuts and bolts of relationships. The command to "love one another" conveys some general advice on how to live, but it's short on specifics regarding the practicalities of human love and how to navigate the twists and turns when things get complicated. Fortunately, such matters are treated elsewhere in the Bible, and they're an important part of what the text has to say about this most basic of human needs.

This chapter considers the birds and the bees in the Bible. The Good Book's view of human sexuality is explored through an examination of passages that treat sex in its various forms and expressions, both "normal" and not so. But we want to be clear about something right off the bat. We're devoting a chapter to this topic not because we're trying to shock or offend our readers or because we're obsessed with sex. (Although we both did come of age during 1967's "summer of love" and therefore are part of a generation whose rallying cry was "Make love, not war.") We include it because it's an essential component of the biblical material that deserves attention and study.

People sometimes pass over or ignore certain parts of the Bible because those sections go against their idea of what should be found in a holy book. But when they do this they're forgetting that the Bible provides insight into every aspect of life, not just spiritual matters and "polite" topics. The text is full of heavenly themes but it's also earthy in many places, sometimes to the point of bawdiness and naughtiness, something we illustrated earlier in chapter 6. And maybe there's a lesson in that for us. Perhaps it's a way of reminding us that the naughty and bawdy can contain an element of the holy.

We begin our discussion with a consideration of the Song of Songs, a work that is unlike any other biblical book because of its exquisite portrayal of desire and sexual longing. We'll then look at a number of biblical romances and hookups, some of them traditional in nature and others less so. A number of practices that might best be termed abnormal or deviant are mentioned in the Bible on occasion and they will be treated as well. This overview will suggest that the Bible's take on human sexuality can't be reduced to a single phrase or a simple aphorism because it's complex and multifaceted. Just like love itself, the Bible's a many splendored thing.

Sex, Not Sexxx

If any biblical book should have a warning label to alert its readers about its contents it's the Song of Songs. It offers a first-person account that describes the thoughts, feelings, and physical effects associated with being head-over-heels in love. Those who stumble upon this book while thumbing through the Bible are in for quite a shock because its intimate and frank portrayal of what love can do to someone is more typical of a diary than a sacred text. But there it sits, right smack in the middle of the Hebrew Bible, a tribute to passion that anyone who has ever been pierced by Cupid's arrow can easily relate to. In other words, it's written for all of us.

Actually, the Song of Songs is tucked away in a relatively obscure corner of the Bible. It's part of a group of books known as the Writings (*ketubim* in Hebrew), a catchall category made up of works that have little in common. In fact, perhaps the most distinguishing trait of the Writings is the incredible range of genres and styles found within the books that comprise it. Among them are Psalms, Proverbs, Job, Ruth, Qohelet (also known as Ecclesiastes), Esther, Daniel, and Chronicles. They represent examples of writings that fall under categories like wisdom, novella, lament, prayer, apocalyptic, and historiography. And, of course, when we throw in the Song of Songs, erotica can be added to the list.

The book is also sometimes known as the Song of Solomon, partly because of several references it makes to the king. As we'll see, the association with Solomon has played a key role in the history of the reception of the book, but actually it appears to have been written long after the reign of David's son and has been dated as late as the third century BCE. This is an example of the practice, common in antiquity, of trying to give written works more legitimacy by ascribing them to prominent individuals even though they didn't write them. In this case, the reference in 1 Kings 4:32 to Solomon having written many songs is an obvious reason why he would be identified with the book. And the fact that he is described elsewhere as quite the ladies' man didn't hurt either (1 Kings 11:1–3).

The Song of Songs is a work of erotic poetry, but we want to be quick to point out that this should not be confused with pornography. It talks a great deal about mutual love, desire, and attraction, but it never explicitly describes sexual intercourse or other ways of physically expressing these feelings. At the same time, there is an egalitarian dimension to the text since both members of the couple share the same longing. It is not exploitative or crude in its treatment of sexuality, and therefore differs significantly from how pornography typically approaches the subject. When speaking about pornography, former Supreme Court Justice Potter Stewart once famously said, "I know it when I see it." The same principle applies to the act of reading. We know pornography when we read it, and the Song of Songs is clearly not pornographic.

The book is a collection of love poems, and scholars disagree over exactly how many separate poems comprise it. It lacks a clear plot, and there is no identifiable structure to the work. The element that unites the entire composition is the theme of love and desire that runs through it. Two voices are clearly discernable in the book, one male and the other female. They are easy to separate out by paying attention to the content of the poems and by virtue of the fact that Hebrew has distinct grammatical forms that indicate masculine or feminine gender. The female voice dominates, as she speaks twelve times and the male speaks eight times. Elsewhere, several voices speak at the same time, and in a few places it is unclear who is doing the speaking. There is not complete agreement among scholars over whether one couple or more than one are present in the text, but most opt for a reading that has one man and one woman as the central figures who are speaking about one another.

The man and woman are not named or identified in any way other than by terms of endearment like "my love/lover." Whoever they are, they have a serious itch that they can't scratch. Like ancient versions of Romeo and Juliet, these star-crossed lovers long to see each other but something is preventing them from being together. What exactly the obstacle is remains unstated. Perhaps a clue is to be found in a refrain that is repeated several times in the book: "Do not stir up or awaken love until it is ready!" (2:7; 3:5; 8:4). Are they too young for romance and being kept apart by overprotective parents? Is one (or both) in another relationship that prevents consummation of theirs? Would their love be frowned upon because they are from different socioeconomic backgrounds? Scholars engage their imaginations (and perhaps sometimes their fantasies) by proposing various scenarios.

The Song of Songs starts off with a verse that calls immediate attention to the book's main theme and sets the tone for an onslaught of sexually charged descriptions and passion-driven declarations that continue unabated for the next eight chapters. "Let him kiss me with the kisses of his mouth!" (1:2) Typical of poetry, the work frequently uses imagery and metaphorical language that is often highly suggestive and full of double entendres. Terms like "anointing oil" (1:3), "fruit" (2:3), and "garden" (4:12) are sometimes used in ways that suggest they are referring to other things than what they usually describe. In some poems these symbolic meanings are clearly spelled out. "You are stately as a palm tree, and your breasts are like its clusters. I say I will climb the palm tree and lay hold of its branches.

O may your breasts be like clusters of the vine, and the scent of your breath like apples, and your kisses like the best wine that goes down smoothly, gliding over lips and teeth" (7:7–8).

In a few passages one of the lovers speaks of the other, calling attention to various body parts and physical traits. In 4:1–7 he compares her eyes to doves, her hair to goats, her teeth to ewes, her cheeks to pomegranates, her breasts to gazelles, and her neck to the tower of David. Keep in mind these are meant to be compliments. They remind us of the vast cultural differences between biblical times and our own: something that might have set someone's heart a-fluttering back then might well result in a slap across the face nowadays. She returns the favor in 5:10–16, where his head is likened to gold, his lips to lilies, his cheeks to beds of spices, his arms to jewels, and his legs to alabaster columns. Despite the odd nature of some of these descriptions they nevertheless offer us some insight into how people of that time imagined beauty and viewed the world around them. By the way, for those interested in a visual representation of what a literal rendering of these descriptions would look like there's a fun image at *http://www.acts17-11.com/snip_song.html*.

The book lacks a narrative, but a few passages are almost story-like and might hint at moments in the couple's relationship or situations they found themselves in. One of the few places they seem to be together is in 5:2–6, a steamy scene that is heavy on the erotic imagery while still leaving much to the imagination.

> I slept, but my heart was awake.
> Listen! My beloved is knocking.
> "Open to me, my sister, my love,
>   my dove, my perfect one;
> for my head is wet with dew,
>   my locks with the drops of the night."
> I had put off my garment;
>   how could I put it on again?
> I had bathed my feet;
>   how could I soil them?
> My beloved thrust his hand into the opening,
>   and my inmost being yearned for him.

I arose to open to my beloved,
and my hands dripped with myrrh,
my fingers with liquid myrrh,
upon the handles of the bolt.
I opened to my beloved,
but my beloved had turned and was gone.

The woman goes on to explain how she looked for her lover but could not find him. As she wanders about the city in search of him the sentinels who guard the walls come upon her and beat her for an undisclosed reason. The section ends with her imploring the "daughters of Jerusalem," a group mentioned elsewhere in the book, to tell her beloved that she is faint with love if they should encounter him.

Scholars disagree on whether passages like this are describing actual events or are better understood to be reports of dreams or fantasies. Did he actually pay her a nighttime visit that ended abruptly before they could consummate their love? Or is this a description of what went through her mind as she spent another sleepless night deprived of the companionship she longed for? The text doesn't provide any clues on how we should read it, but however it's interpreted we're left with a vivid portrayal of the all-consuming nature of love and desire.

So how does a work like this end up in the Bible? That's a great question, especially when we keep in mind that God isn't mentioned a single time in the Song of Songs. Apparently, those who had to make the decision on it had similar questions. Tradition tells us that it was one of the last books accepted into the canon of the Hebrew Bible and there was quite a bit of resistance to its inclusion. A number of factors played a role in helping it make the cut, one of which was its references to Solomon, mentioned earlier, that caused Bible scholars of prior generations to assume he was its author. Since other works associated with him, like Proverbs, had already made the grade, the Song of Songs was viewed favorably.

Another thing that was instrumental in tipping the scales was the long history of reading the book as an allegory, a work whose surface meaning needs to be read symbolically to discover the deeper, hidden truths it contains. In this case, interpreters often assumed that even though Song of Songs doesn't mention God it's really about God. The man and the woman represent God and Israel, and the love between them is symbolic of the covenant that unites the two. A similar interpretive move was made in the Christian community, where the couple and their passion personify Jesus and his love for the church or for individual Christians. In this way, a text that appears to be devoid of theological significance is "rehabilitated" and made more relevant for faith purposes. Allegorical reading of the Bible has had a long history in both Judaism and Christianity, but it has been viewed more cautiously in recent times because it tends to ignore or downplay the apparent meaning of a text while introducing new meanings that have no textual support.

However Song of Songs made it into the Bible, we're glad it's there. Without it, the Judeo-Christian tradition would be deprived of one of the greatest reflections on love in world literature, ancient or modern. Even if it doesn't mention God, it uses humanity's shared experience of love to teach transcendent and eternal truths that shouldn't be forgotten.

> Set me as a seal upon your heart
>> as a seal upon your arm;
> for love is strong as death,
>> passion fierce as the grave.
> Its flashes are flashes of fire,
>> a raging flame.
> Many waters cannot quench love,
>> neither can floods drown it.
> If one offered for love
>> all the wealth of his house,
>> it would be utterly scorned. (8:6–7)

We say "Amen!" to that.

Two's Company, Three's a Crowd

In addition to the anonymous lovers in Song of Songs, there are a number of other biblical characters who become all starry-eyed and weak-kneed under the power of love. Among them are three we'll discuss here whose amorous adventures lead to less than happy results for either themselves or the objects of their affection. The first is the wife of Joseph's Egyptian master Potiphar, who finds herself overly attracted to the newest addition to the household staff. The story is told in Genesis 39 after Joseph has been sold into Egypt by his brothers, who were jealous of Joseph's status as their father Jacob's favorite son.

It begins with the observation that Joseph was the kind of guy who could turn the ladies' heads: "Now Joseph was handsome and good-looking" (Gen. 39:6b). Because the text rarely calls attention to their physical appearance, it's amazing how little we know about what the people mentioned in the Bible actually looked like. Occasionally we get descriptions of them, though, and when we do we should sit up and take notice. A good rule of thumb when reading the Bible is to pay extra attention to any physical description of a character, no matter how seemingly insignificant or subtle. It could be a reference to a body part, a trait, or a defect. Don't forget it, because nine times out of ten it's going to factor into the plot. The present passage is an excellent example of how this works. After we're told that Joseph is a looker, the very next verse turns up the heat. "And after a time his master's wife cast her eyes on Joseph and said, 'Lie with me.'"

He rebuffs her but she doesn't take "No!" for an answer, and the text says that "day after day" she tried to seduce him. After one encounter she grabs Joseph's garment and he leaves it in her hand as he flees. With that physical evidence she's able to manufacture trumped-up charges that Joseph tried to attack her but she was able to fend him off, and this is the story she tells Potiphar when he returns home. Her husband falls for it, hook, line, and sinker, and he has Joseph thrown into prison for a crime he didn't commit. The story has a happy ending when Joseph is released from jail by the Pharaoh and rises to the rank of second-in-command in Egypt, but he still had to serve hard time because his master's wife couldn't keep her hands off him.

The gender roles are reversed in the story of one of the most famous couples in biblical literature, Samson and Delilah, whose story is found in Judges 16. Many readers assume that Samson and Delilah were married, but that wasn't the case. In fact, while the text says that he loved her, it never states that she felt the same way.

He appears to have been smitten quite badly because he eventually breaks down and tells her that his long hair (reader alert—another physical description!) is the source of his strength, even though he puts himself in harm's way by tipping her off. She's able to pry this secret out of him by employing the oldest trick in the book of lovers: the guilt trip. "How can you say, 'I love you,' when your heart is not with me? You have mocked me three times now and have not told me what makes your strength so great" (Judg. 16:15). Samson was no Joseph. After Delilah pestered him "day after day," he told her the truth, thus guaranteeing himself a seat in the barber's chair. Like Joseph, he ends up in prison, but Samson's story also has a happy ending—of sorts. Though he is blinded by the Philistines who captured him, his hair begins to grow back and in a final act of revenge he manages to collapse the house, killing himself and thousands of his enemies. Perhaps he was reevaluating his relationship with Delilah as the roof caved in.

Our third coupling involves King David and Bathsheba, whose relationship begins in 2 Samuel 11. The chapter describes a royal screwup in which the king falls for the wife of another man. David spies Bathsheba, wife of Uriah, from his roof as she is bathing, and the alert reader who is always on the lookout for physical descriptions (we mean you) knows romance is around the corner because Bathsheba is described as "very beautiful" (2 Sam. 11:2). David summons her to the palace for a tryst, and Bathsheba becomes pregnant. Once he learns of the pregnancy, the king's problems are compounded by the fact that Uriah is off fighting in a war that David himself should be leading. He summons Uriah back home in the hope that he will sleep with his wife and assume the child is his, but the loyal soldier refuses to do so, proclaiming, "The ark and Israel and Judah remain in booths; and my lord Joab and the servants of my lord are camping in the open field; shall I then go to my house to eat and to drink, and to lie with my wife? As you live and as your soul lives, I will not do such a thing" (11:11). Demonstrating how low some commanders-in-chief will go, David sends Uriah back to war unwittingly carrying his own death warrant, a letter from David ordering that he be sent to the front lines where he'll be killed. And it isn't long before Bathsheba is packing up her things and moving into the palace.

The pattern holds here, too, as tragedy leads to good fortune. Just when David thinks he's dodged a bullet and gotten off scot-free, God's spokesman, in the person of the prophet Nathan, knocks on his door to denounce his actions in l'affaire Bathsheba. In a delicious scene of self-entrapment Nathan tells David a parable that results in David condemning himself (2 Sam. 12). Touché! Even the mighty monarch has to play by God's rules and isn't above the law. David and Bathsheba's son dies soon after birth but the next child born to the couple will be Solomon, who succeeds his father on the throne and rules over a time of great prosperity for Israel. Still, we can't help but wonder how much sleep David lost due to his wandering eye and untamed heart.

All three of these relationships underscore the wisdom of the refrain, repeated three times in the Song of Songs, that advises, "Do not stir up or awaken love until it is ready!" The stories of Potiphar's wife, Samson, and David all issue a warning against unbridled passion and illustrate how the wheels can come off when infatuation and lust consume a person. In the world of the Bible, desire and sexual feelings are good things when expressed properly and channeled in the right direction. But in other situations they must be carefully held in check, or problems arise and people get hurt. Some things never change.

Before leaving this topic, we'd like to discuss some romantic relationships mentioned in the Bible that are unique because they have more than two partners. The first is that involving Abraham, Sarah, and Hagar, described in several places in Genesis 16–21. When his wife Sarah is unable to conceive, she suggests that Abraham take her maidservant Hagar so that he might have children through her. As the story unfolds both women eventually have a son, with Ishmael being born to Hagar and Isaac to Sarah.

The other grouping includes Jacob, Leah, and Rachel, whose relationships are described in Genesis 29–31. Their situation is complicated by a couple of factors. The first is the relationship the two women have to one another and to Jacob. They are sisters who are also Jacob's cousins, reflecting the practice of endogamy, or marriage within the family, that was common in antiquity and is still found in some places today. The second is the role played by Bilhah and Zilpah, the maidservants of Rachel and Leah respectively. Similar to what occurs between Abraham and Hagar, Bilhah and Zilpah are given to Jacob by their mistresses when it appears that Rachel and Leah are unable to have children. The twelve sons of Jacob, the ancestors of the twelve tribes of Israel, are born to these four women.

We treated these stories in an earlier chapter from one angle, but here we're focusing on a different aspect of them. Both these sets of relationships share certain features in common. One is the presence of what is referred to as the "barren wife" motif. Sarah and Rachel give their maidservants to Abraham and Jacob because they are unable to have children. This situation, yet another example of a physical description, in this case apparent infertility, occurs with several other women in the Hebrew Bible, and in each case the woman soon becomes pregnant through divine intervention. This relates to the important role of lineage in both of these sets of relationships, a second feature these stories share: all center on continuation of the family line so that the covenant with God can be passed on to future generations. A further thing they have in common is that a bit of tension exists between the women in these relationships. When Hagar conceives she looks down on her mistress Sarah with contempt (Gen. 16:4), and twice Sarah manages to drive her maidservant from the family home (Gen. 16:6; 21:10). Similarly, Leah accuses Rachel of taking her husband from her, suggesting a strain in the relationship between the two sisters (Gen. 30:15). Like the hit HBO series *Big Love* about the multiple marriages of a Mormon man living in Utah, these passages describe the inevitable problems that arise between individuals who are vying for the attention and affection of the same person.

The Dark Side

We all come to realize, usually around the time of our first crush, that being physically attracted to another person is a two-edged sword. On the one hand, it can fill us with thoughts and feelings we never had before and lead us to do things we normally wouldn't dream of attempting. Many great works of art and feats of daring (as well as monumental flops) have had their origin in or been motivated by the power of love. As the song says, "Ain't no mountain high enough." But then there's the flip side. Sometimes, as the other song says,

"Love hurts." It can hurt both the person in love and the one who is the object of a person's love. As creative as love can be, it also holds the potential to be destructive. There's bound to be some of both in any normal relationship but on occasion the destructive element dominates, and that's when things can get ugly.

The Bible is well aware of this double dimension to human desire, and it acknowledges the problems that can result when passion is expressed in harmful or unhealthy ways. One of the most tragic stories in the entire Bible is found in 2 Samuel 13, which describes how David's son Amnon rapes his own half-sister Tamar. It's a painful story to read, and not just because of the nature of the act it describes. The narrator gives us a glimpse into Amnon's mind both before and after the rape, presenting a disturbing description of how obsession can transform into hatred. As the story begins, Amnon is so tormented by his love for his half-sister that he has made himself sick. After he forces himself on Tamar he begins to despise her and banishes her from his presence. "Indeed, his loathing was even greater than the lust he had felt for her" (2 Sam. 13:15). The portrayal of Tamar is heartrending. She pleads with Amnon to leave her alone to no avail, and after the rape she is shattered, distraught, and alone. "So Tamar remained, a desolate woman, in her brother Absalom's house" (2 Sam. 13:20). It's the Bible's most eloquent cautionary tale about the devastating effects of unbridled sexual longing.

Some of the biblical laws attempt to regulate behavior in sexual matters. Leviticus 18:6–18 contains a long list of forbidden sexual partners as a way of defining what constitutes incest. This is followed by a prohibition against sexual intercourse during menstruation. A bit later the chapter lists regulations against bestiality that are directed to both men and women. It goes without saying that these laws exist because certain people were engaging in these activities and they needed to be held in check. The text says that these practices pollute and defile the land, and that's why they are outlawed (Lev. 18:24–30).

Also nestled in Leviticus 18 is the Hebrew Bible's clearest reference to homosexuality (Lev. 18:22), a prohibition that is directed to men. This text and certain others have been cited frequently by those who claim the Bible is opposed to homosexuality. In the chapter on geography we explained why the Sodom and Gomorrah story in

Genesis 19 shouldn't be read in this way because it is primarily concerned with hospitality, not sexuality. In Leviticus 18 the situation is different because its topic is sexual. This has led some to see the passage as a prohibition against homosexuality that is relevant for all times and places. But this is much too simplistic an approach to adopt for such an important issue. Ancient notions of sexuality and attitudes toward it differed significantly from our own, and it would be a mistake to take our own understanding and impose it on the biblical text. In addition, study of the vocabulary used in passages that are cited in the homosexuality discussion reveals subtle nuances and shades of meaning that can significantly change how they should be translated into another language like English. For example, both 1 Corinthians 6:9–10 and 1 Timothy 1:9–11 contain a list of various types of sinners and each list has a word that has been sometimes translated as "homosexual," "sodomite," and even "pervert." But New Testament scholars have become increasingly skeptical about giving such a meaning to the word. When viewed in the wider context of Greco-Roman culture and literature it is clear that the term does not describe a particular sexual orientation, but rather refers to a sexual relationship that is exploitative in nature regardless of whether or not the people involved are of the same gender. Words only mean something in context, and when the context isn't our own, things can get complicated.

Finally, there's the issue of using biblical law to determine what's right and wrong in our day and age. Do we really want to go down that road? Where and how should we draw the line on what's relevant and what's not? Should all laws in the Bible inform our legal system? If so, check out Exodus 21:17 and its implications. That would definitely be one way to thin the human herd.

Jesus, the Love Guru

Compared to the Hebrew Bible, the New Testament's treatment of love is quite tame. There are no steamy passages that describe sexual longing like those in Song of Songs, and we don't find gut-wrenching stories about lust run amuck like that of Amnon and Tamar. Still, the subject does not go unaddressed in the Christian scriptures, and the New Testament adds a few nuances to the Bible's overall view of one of humanity's favorite topics and pastimes. Perhaps the New Testament's most well-known passage on the subject is found in 1 Corinthians 13, Paul's ode to love that ends with the statement that love stands supreme beside its fellow virtues of faith and hope. The passage is frequently read at weddings, and any bride or groom (or anyone else in attendance, for that matter) who takes the time to reflect on the words as they're being spoken can't help but be moved by them. And while we second the emotion, it's worth taking into consideration that Paul's words also have a context. He's describing what love is for the benefit of the people in the church at Corinth because at least some of them are exhibiting exactly the opposite qualities. That's not to say that patience, kindness, and the rest aren't ingredients in the recipe of love. But Paul's "definition" isn't an abstract one; it's aimed at correcting the behavior of a specific audience.

Jesus' teachings often mention love, and one of his famous utterances on the subject came in response to a man who asked him what the greatest commandment in the law is (Matt. 22:34–39). Drawing on Deuteronomy 6:5, Jesus responded that loving God with your whole heart, soul, and mind is the number-one commandment. The text mentions that the questioner was a lawyer, and so he probably considered himself to be an authority on the subject. Perhaps that's why Jesus couldn't resist throwing in a little free legal advice of his own by identifying what he considered to be the second greatest commandment. Citing Leviticus 19:18 this time, he instructs the man, "You shall love your neighbor as yourself."

We all know how hard it can be to follow that command, but its degree of difficulty pales in comparison to another one Jesus issues earlier in Matthew's Gospel. It's well known that Jesus had a penchant for speaking in parables and riddles that would often leave his listeners wrestling with the implications of his words, but this one's a real head-scratcher that seems to fly in the face of common sense and human nature. In the middle of the Sermon on the Mount, Jesus lists a number of ways that the law needs to be reimagined, and one of them has to do with love. "You have heard that it was said, 'You shall love your neighbor and hate your enemy.' But I say to you, Love your enemies and pray for those who persecute you" (Matt. 5:43–44).

Jesus has just instructed his audience to turn the other cheek when they're struck (Matt. 5:39), but this advice dramatically ups the ante. It's a completely new way of thinking about the nature and purpose of love that highlights how revolutionary his thinking was, and Christians everywhere continue to struggle to keep up with his message and put it into practice.

13 The Bible Recycled

Sample This

One day a number of years back we had an interesting experience as we were driving to a book club meeting. A song came on the radio that started with a guitar riff we immediately recognized as the beginning of *Ventura Highway*, a huge hit for the band America in the early 1970s. But within fifteen seconds it abruptly morphed into something completely different that we had never heard before. Instead of the familiar male voice we remembered from our college days singing immortal lines like "alligator lizards in the air," a female voice began to sing another set of lyrics to an entirely different melody. The song went on for about four and a half minutes, and for most of that time the guitar part from *Ventura Highway* could be plainly picked out. We later learned that the song was *Someone to Call My Lover* by Janet Jackson, which went on to become so popular it earned her a Grammy nomination.

We bring this up not to reveal anything about our musical tastes, as stuck-in-the-'70s as they might be. This little story actually relates directly to an aspect of the Bible that often goes unnoticed or unappreciated. Janet Jackson (or her producer) was sampling, a practice that has a long and distinguished history in music. Sometimes musicians will take something from another artist's work and use it in their own songs. It might be a snippet of notes or words, or it could be a longer section of material taken from the original composition. Sometimes, as in *Someone to Call My Lover*, the borrowed section becomes a core element of the new work that continues or is repeated throughout it, and at other times it's used only briefly. As you might imagine, the legal issues associated with sampling can be dicey and sometimes an artist whose work too closely resembles another's will be taken to court, as former Beatle George Harrison learned after a lawsuit involving his song *My Sweet Lord.* (Yep, we're stuck in the '70s.)

Luckily, copyright laws did not exist in antiquity. If they had been around then, many biblical authors would have been in hot water because the ancient equivalent of sampling pops up frequently throughout the Bible. In some cases, the biblical literature is obviously dependent upon written sources from other cultures and contexts, like Mesopotamia and Egypt. This would be the equivalent of Janet Jackson drawing from classical music sources, which she in fact did in *Someone to Call My Lover.* Parts of her song are based on the piece *Gymnopédie No. 1*, by the late-nineteenth-century composer Eric Satie, making Jackson a double sampler. At other times, the biblical authors stayed closer to home and reused material from other books in the canon or, in some cases, the works those books were drawing on.

The analogy with sampling isn't perfect, but it's a helpful way to think about how some parts of the Bible took shape. Like musicians, authors of written works can recycle material from other sources and use it for their own purposes to create something new. That's what's behind the latest craze in "mash-up" literature like *Pride and Prejudice and Zombies*, a book that rewrites the Jane Austen classic novel by adding brain-eating zombies to it. When they recycle a passage or theme and adapt it to fit another literary or social context the biblical writers are doing something similar, only without the zombies.

The Gospel Truth

The Gospels are an ideal place to begin our exploration of the phenomenon of biblical sampling. As the New Testament writings that contain the most information about the life of Jesus, the four Gospels have been read and revered by Christians for nearly twenty centuries. Portions of them are proclaimed in churches every day, and many people turn to them for spiritual, moral, and practical guidance on how to live. It's no exaggeration to say that the Gospels are among the most influential works of literature ever written—even more influential than the Harry Potter books.

For most of the history of the Gospels the focus of attention was on their message and content, not their backgrounds. This was also true of the way people related to the Bible as a whole. All of that changed in the eighteenth century, with the rise of critical study of the Bible, when scholars began to examine issues like the contexts the various books emerged from and responded to, how the texts were composed and transmitted, and the relationships among the different biblical writings. This approach revolutionized how the Bible was studied, and it ushered in new ways of thinking about an old book.

As these new methods of critical study developed, the Gospels were a natural place for scholars to turn their attention. Even the most cursory reading of the four books raises some important questions. While they all appear to have the same aim—to present Jesus' life story—each does so in a different way. The Gospels share much in common, but there's also a great deal that's distinct about each one. Even in those places where they seem to be telling the same story, it's never presented in exactly the same way. On top of that, three of the Gospels—Matthew, Mark, and Luke—appear to be much closer to one another than to John, a Gospel chock-full of stories and traditions about Jesus not found in the other three.

Similarities among the first three Gospels led scholars to identify Matthew, Mark, and Luke as the "Synoptic Gospels," *synoptic* from a Greek word that means "see together." A major mystery related to these works is referred to as the "Synoptic Problem," which seeks to understand and explain the literary and historical relationships that exist among the first three Gospels. The most widely accepted solution to the Synoptic Problem is the "two-source hypothesis," which can be summarized as follows. Mark is the shortest Gospel, and much of its contents are found in both Matthew and Luke. This suggests that Mark was the first Gospel written, and Matthew and Luke somehow used Mark to assist them in writing their Gospels. There is an additional set of material that is shared by Matthew and Luke but not found in Mark. The simplest explanation for this is that those two Gospels had access to a second source that either was unavailable to Mark or he chose not to use in his Gospel. An interesting feature about the material shared by Matthew and Luke is that it's all in the form of sayings of Jesus, with no miracle stories or other narratives. Bible scholars refer to this source by the letter "Q," an abbreviation of the German *Quelle*, which means "source." (Many of the pioneers of modern biblical scholarship were, like early brewmasters, German-speaking.) It should be noted that an actual, physical Q source does not exist; rather, Q is a theoretical construct of Bible scholars that helps explain how it is that Matthew and Luke share material that's not in Mark.

Mark and Q are the two sources at the heart of the two-source hypothesis, but they don't explain all the passages in the Synoptic Gospels. In addition, both Matthew and Luke have stories and other material that are found only in their Gospels. For example, the infancy narratives that treat Jesus' conception and birth and which were discussed in an earlier chapter are found in only the first two chapters of Matthew and Luke, and they share virtually nothing in common. This indicates that the authors of these two Gospels had access to traditions that were unavailable to the other Gospel writers, and scholars designate these sources as "M" and "L." In this way, the various literary relationships among the three Synoptic Gospels are explained and accounted for, in theory at least.

In the remainder of this section we consider a few examples of biblical recycling in the Gospels. These examples are illustrative of the phenomenon and could be multiplied many times over since each Gospel frequently draws upon non-Gospel biblical books or reworks material found in one or more of the other Gospels.

A distinctive feature of Matthew's Gospel is its heavy concentration of "fulfillment citations," in which the author connects certain events of Jesus' life with passages from the writings of the prophets in the Hebrew Bible. This is usually done by first describing the event and then using some variation of the formula "this happened to fulfill what was spoken of by the prophet X," followed by a quotation from a prophetic writing. Scholars disagree on the exact number of these fulfillment citations in Matthew, with the figure varying between ten and twelve. (As you've probably picked up by now, Bible scholars disagree on many things.) By contrast, John has five of them and Mark and Luke contain just a few each.

These citations are found throughout Matthew's Gospel, but five of them are found in the first two chapters that comprise the infancy narrative. Matthew uses those five quotations to explain why Jesus is conceived (1:23); why he's born in Bethlehem (2:6); why Joseph, Mary, and Jesus go to Egypt (2:15); why Herod kills the innocent children (2:18); and why Jesus is called a Nazorean (2:23). In the rest of the Gospel they help explain why Jesus settles in Capernaum (4:15–16); why he performs so many healings (8:17); why he prefers not to be known publicly (12:17–21); why he speaks in parables (13:35); why he enters Jerusalem on a donkey and a colt (21:4–5); and why a burial ground is purchased with the money Judas returns to the Jewish authorities (27:9–10).

In all likelihood Matthew uses fulfillment citations so frequently because he is writing to a Christian community whose members are mostly Jewish, and who would find reassurance in the knowledge that the earlier prophets were writing about Jesus. And so Matthew sprinkles references to the prophetic writings throughout his Gospel in an effort to reassure his audience that Jesus is the promised Messiah. The presence of these familiar passages in this new context functions as a running thread throughout the Gospel that's meant to remind the reader that the events being described come under God's control and are all part of the divine plan. In other words, the recycled prophetic texts serve a powerful rhetorical purpose in the First Gospel by interpreting the events of Jesus' life in light of the writings of the past.

Recycling sometimes takes place within and among the Gospels. The four books share things in common but no two of them ever present a story in exactly the same way. Sometimes the same passage is found in different places in different Gospels. An example of this can be seen with the placement of Jesus' genealogy in Matthew and Luke, the only two Gospels to mention his family line. Matthew begins his Gospel with a listing of Jesus' family tree before he's even born (1:1–17), while Luke doesn't introduce it until Jesus is baptized as an adult (3:23–38). In addition, a comparison of those texts shows some striking differences in the ways the two lists are arranged and the names they contain.

Elsewhere, elements within the same story are sometimes reworked or modified. All three Synoptic Gospels describe a scene in which Jesus and his disciples are in a boat on the Sea of Galilee when a storm arises. While he is asleep the wind threatens to capsize the boat, so the disciples awaken Jesus and beg him to save them. According to Mark (4:35–41) and Luke (8:22–25), Jesus first calms the storm and then rebukes the disciples for their lack of faith. In Matthew's version of the story the order is the opposite—Jesus first reprimands the disciples, and then he calms the storm (8:23–27). It's a subtle change, but it fits Matthew's purposes to have Jesus give the lesson in discipleship before performing the miracle.

Another interesting example of how the Gospels present the same material in different ways is seen in the Sermon on the Mount, the most famous speech Jesus gives in the New Testament. It's found in chapters 5 through 7 of Matthew's Gospel, and it has often been referred to as the quintessential summary of Jesus' teaching. No other Gospel describes the scene, but Luke has Jesus give a speech that has many connections with the Sermon on the Mount (Luke 6:20–49). In Luke Jesus speaks to the crowds not on a mount but on a "level place" (6:17), although in the previous scene Jesus had been on a mountain (6:12). For this reason the Luke text is often referred to as the "Sermon on the Plain."

The lengths of the two speeches are dramatically different: in Matthew, Jesus goes on for more than one hundred verses, while Luke's speech is only twenty-nine verses long. But the form and content of the speeches suggest they are two related versions that draw upon the same material and are organized in a similar fashion. For example, both begin with a listing of the beatitudes ("Blessed are the poor . . ."), and both end with a parable describing two men, one who builds his house on solid ground and one who doesn't. Similarly, most of the content of Luke's speech is found in the Sermon on the Mount or elsewhere in Matthew's Gospel.

Nonetheless, there are important differences between the Sermon on the Mount and the Sermon on the Plain beyond their altitudes and lengths. For example, the Beatitudes are expressed somewhat differently, as the first one of the series suggests. Matthew begins his with "Blessed are the poor in spirit" (5:3), while Luke has "Blessed are you who are poor" (6:20). All nine of Matthew's beatitudes except the last one are presented in the third person, while Luke has only four and they are all in the second person. In addition,

Luke follows up his Beatitudes with a list of four "woes" that condemn people who are rich, full, laughing, and well spoken of, but Matthew doesn't include anything like this.

Similar material is used in each speech—much of it probably from the Q source—but it has been adapted and reworked to suit the focus and agenda of each author. Matthew's Gospel depicts Jesus as a Moses-like figure in a number of ways. At his birth he escapes from a foreign-born ruler who demands that all male children under a certain age be put to death. Joseph, Mary, and Jesus flee to Egypt and eventually leave there to return to Palestine. There are clear echoes of the Moses story in those and other scenes. The Sermon on the Mount also recalls Moses in some important ways. Its setting on a mountain and the heavy emphasis it places on the law (5:17–48) are reminiscent of Moses receiving the law on Mt. Sinai. The connection Matthew tries to draw between Moses and Jesus in these and other passages once again reflects the Jewish makeup of his audience, for whom Moses is a venerated figure.

By contrast, Luke's Sermon on the Plain makes no reference to the law, reflecting the likely Gentile composition of his audience. It is often remarked that Luke's Gospel is a relatively egalitarian one as seen, for example, in the important role women play in many places within it. It might also be why Luke adopts the more personal second person "you" in his Beatitudes. However we understand the connections between Matthew's and Luke's portrayals of this important discourse by Jesus, there is no denying that they are based on a common tradition and sources that have been shaped into two distinct but related stories.

We don't want to ignore John's Gospel completely so we'll briefly mention a couple of ways that he contributes to the biblical recycling project. As already noted, there is very little overlap between John and the Synoptic Gospels. The Fourth Gospel has a distinct vocabulary, and most of its stories are not found in Matthew, Mark, or Luke. And even in those few places where there is agreement among all of them, John typically puts his distinct spin on things. For example, all four Gospels contain a story that is sometimes referred to as the "cleansing of the Temple," in which Jesus chases people engaged in business transactions out of the sacred precinct. This story is found toward the end of the Synoptic Gospels, when Jesus enters

Jerusalem for the last time before he is arrested and put to death (Matt. 21:12–3; Mark 11:15–17; Luke 19:45–46). But John places it much earlier, at the beginning of his Gospel when Jesus' career is just getting started (2:13–17). He also throws in a reference to Jesus using a whip to clear out the Temple area, à la Indiana Jones, a detail not found in the other three Gospels. As we saw in an earlier chapter, John has a different chronology for the Last Supper, and we see another example of that here in the temple-cleansing scene. When it comes to more profound differences regarding how Jesus is presented, it's clear that in comparison to the other Gospels John has what is sometimes referred to by New Testament scholars as a "high Christology." This is seen in the titles John uses for Jesus and the words of Jesus himself, which highlight his unique relationship with God.

John is much more interested in Jesus' origins than his three fellow evangelists. We've already mentioned that Matthew and Luke are the only Gospels that list Jesus' family tree, with Matthew tracing his roots to Abraham and Luke going all the way back to Adam. John does them one better by presenting Jesus as the preexistent Word who is equal to God and the source of all that exists. This idea is introduced at the very beginning of his Gospel in a prologue found in the book's first eighteen verses.

Many commentators have pointed out a similarity between the way John opens his Gospel ("In the beginning was the Word . . .") and the first words of the book of Genesis ("In the beginning . . ."). It's likely the author of John is alluding to the Bible's first book, but the content of his prologue is actually heavily indebted to Greek thought and philosophical traditions. In fact, scholars believe John may be recycling a preexistent Greek composition that he modified to become a hymn about the preexistent Word of God. A point in favor of that view is the fact that the prologue does not mention Jesus by name until the very end, suggesting that the piece originally served some other purpose before Jesus was introduced as an add-on.

This brief overview indicates that there is strong evidence the Gospels often rework and recycle material that is taken from both the biblical writings and other literature. That editorial activity was undertaken to articulate and support each Gospel's unique Christology, or understanding of who Jesus was. Matthew depicts a Jewish messiah, while John has the preexistent Word of God, and Mark and Luke present markedly different visions of Jesus as well. These various Christologies are sometimes expressed through a creative reinterpretation of sources and traditions. Similar to Janet Jackson's use of *Ventura Highway*, the original text is then transformed and experienced in a whole new way.

In with the Old

The books of the Hebrew Bible also sometimes show familiarity with or dependence upon other sources that are adapted to fit their new literary contexts. One of the clearest examples of this is the flood narrative of Genesis 6–9. The story of Noah is part of the primeval history found in the first eleven chapters of the Bible that contain myths meant to explain things like the creation of the world (Gen. 1–3), the first homicide (the Cain and Abel story), and the origin of the various languages people speak (the Tower of Babel story). The flood narrative, which describes how only Noah's family and a few animals survived a deluge sent by God, is the longest portion of the primeval history.

You'd be hard-pressed to find a culture that doesn't have a flood story. They're found all over the world, and while some of them appear to be related the details can differ wildly from one place to another. For example, it's difficult to reconcile the story from Cameroon about a brother and sister who escape a flood with the help of a talking goat and the Australian one about a god who becomes so angry with humanity that he creates a flood by urinating into the ocean. Sometimes there are striking similarities between the flood stories of different cultures, especially neighboring ones, and this can suggest possible contact or influence of one on another. That's the case with the biblical flood story and several others that come from Mesopotamia.

A Sumerian text from about 2000 BCE has King Ziusudra escape a seven-day flood in a boat, while an Akkadian tale dating to 1700 BCE describes how the god Enki warns Atrahasis to build a boat so he can ride out a storm sent by other gods who are angry with humanity and wish to destroy all people. There are also some interesting parallels between the Genesis flood story and the Gilgamesh epic. That eighteenth-century BCE work describes how a man named Utnapishtim builds a boat, survives a flood, sends out birds to determine when the dry land reappears, and offers sacrifices to gods when he is back on dry land. These actions mirror closely what Noah does in Genesis 6–9, suggesting that the author of the biblical text is sampling Gilgamesh, which itself could be sampling Atrahasis.

The parallels between the biblical flood story and those from other parts of the ancient Near East show that the biblical author was familiar with those other traditions and drew upon them to compose the Genesis account. The influence could not have gone in the opposite direction because the Mesopotamian texts are centuries older than the biblical one and were well established by the time Genesis reached its final form. As with the Gospel passages mentioned earlier, this recycling of earlier material is done in a way that supports the author's agenda and reflects its biblical context. In this case the flood story ends with an articulation of the covenant that exists between God and humanity, which is the first mention of this concept, which is central to the Hebrew Bible (9:8–17).

The flood story reflects a belief in God's supremacy over the forces of nature. In some ancient Near Eastern cultures this same idea is sometimes expressed in descriptions of battles between a god and elements of the natural world that are personified as other deities. This can be seen in the Baal cycle, a set of mythological texts from around 1400 BCE that were found in modern Syria in the 1940s at the site of the ancient city of Ugarit. According to the Ugaritic myth, Baal, a storm god, battles and overcomes Yamm, the god of the sea, to become king of the gods.

The Bible does not refer specifically to the battle between Baal and Yamm, but certain texts that refer to Yahweh defeating the sea (*yam*, in Hebrew) contain echoes of this motif. A number of psalms refer to this encounter that demonstrates God's authority over the waters. "O LORD God of hosts, who is as mighty as you, O LORD? Your faithfulness surrounds you. You rule the raging of the sea; when its waves rise, you still them. You crushed Rahab like a carcass; you scattered your enemies with your mighty arm" (Ps. 89:8–10; cf. 24:1–2; 74:12–15; 93:1–5). Some passages, like this one, have God overcome the dragon or sea monster known as Rahab (Job 26:12), and elsewhere reference is made to another sea serpent known as Leviathan: "On that day the LORD with his cruel and great and strong sword will punish Leviathan the fleeing serpent, Leviathan the twisting serpent, and he will kill the dragon that is in the sea" (Isa. 27:1; cf. Job 3:8). This same sea monster, in a variant spelling ("Litan"), is defeated by Baal in a much older Ugaritic text: "You smote Litan the twisting serpent, made an end of the crooked serpent, the tyrant with the seven heads."[1] Such texts show that the biblical authors are familiar with the theme of a god who defeats chaos and the forces of nature, as was found in the literature of neighboring cultures, and they sometimes used this motif in their descriptions of the God of Israel.

The "recycling center" of the Bible might very well be Proverbs 22:17–24:22. This section, titled "the words of the wise," looks very much like what is found throughout the rest of the book. The passage is full of advice and admonitions of the sort that a parent might pass on to a child or a teacher to a student. But in this instance the teacher is guilty of plagiarism because a significant portion of the section appears to have been lifted from another work from a completely different culture. At least twenty-two of its eighty-six verses bear a striking resemblance to what is found in a much older Egyptian composition (eleventh or twelfth century BCE) known as the "Instruction of Amenemope." Virtually all Bible scholars believe the biblical author responsible for this section of the book of Proverbs borrowed directly from the Egyptian work.

The similarities between the two texts are most likely not coincidental, a phenomenon sometimes described by the fancy term "polygenesis." It's one thing if a word of advice like "do unto others as you would have them do unto you" pops up in more than one place (and it does; that's a sentiment found in various forms in a wide variety of cultures throughout history). But that isn't what we have here. "The words of the wise" in Proverbs and the "Instruction of Amenemope" share a great many axioms in common, and some of them treat topics much more offbeat than the Golden Rule. For example,

---

[1] Quoted in John Day, "Leviathan," in *The Anchor Bible Dictionary*, ed. David Noel Freedman (New York: Doubleday, 1992), 4:295–96.

they both explain how to eat in the presence of an important person (Prov. 23:1–3), prohibit the removal of landmarks (23:10), and discuss the finer points of vomiting (23:6–8). In addition, Proverbs makes a cryptic reference to "thirty sayings" (22:20), which could be an indirect reference to the thirty chapters in the "Instruction of Amenemope," since there are way more than thirty sayings in "the words of the wise." All indications are that this is the Bible's example of sampling *par excellence*.

Come Out, Come Out, Wherever You Are!

For ancient Israelites and modern Jews, the Exodus has loomed large as a foundational event that has shaped the community's self-identity and understanding of its relationship with God. The description of the flight from Egypt and crossing of the Red (probably "Reed") Sea in Exodus 13–14, followed by a forty-year period of wandering in the wilderness before entering the promised land, is familiar to all Bible readers. It is cherished by those who see in it God's concern and love for the Israelites, but at the same time it serves as a warning of the consequences that await those who give in to temptation and disobey God's word.

Given its importance, it should come as no surprise that the Exodus is often alluded to in other parts of the Hebrew Bible. Historical books, legal texts, prophetic writings, and psalms all cite the Exodus to highlight God's role in rescuing the Israelites from oppression and to remind people to behave in a way that is worthy of such divine favor. It therefore serves as an excellent example of how a biblical tradition can be reused in a variety of literary and social contexts.

One of the most interesting uses of the Exodus motif is found in Second Isaiah. Chapters 40–55 of the book of Isaiah are commonly referred to as "Second Isaiah" because they appear to have been written at a later time than the book's first thirty-nine chapters. Whereas the first section of the book probably comes from the eighth century BCE, when Assyria was the dominant power in the ancient Near East, the portion beginning with chapter 40 is responding to events in the sixth century BCE when Babylon was calling the shots. Second Isaiah is directed to those Israelites who had been deported from their land and were now living in Babylon during a period known as the Babylonian Exile, which lasted from 586 until 538.

To comfort those in exile and give them a sense of hope, Second Isaiah interprets their situation in light of the Exodus. Just as God brought their ancestors out of Egypt, guided them through the wilderness, and brought them into their own land, so too will those in Babylon be brought back home (Isa. 43:5). Second Isaiah conveys this message of hope through a series of arresting images that recall the events of the Exodus and what took place after it. Their present circumstances, as difficult as they might be, are an opportunity for them to experience a divine intervention as dramatic and miraculous as what occurred centuries earlier when the Israelites fled Pharaoh and his forces as God parted the waters for them. "When you pass through the waters, I will be with you; and through the rivers, they shall not overwhelm you" (Isa. 43:2a; cf. 42:15). As God provided for the Israelites who wandered in the wilderness, so God will provide water for those in exile as they make their journey home. "For I give water in the wilderness, rivers in the desert, to give drink to my chosen people" (Isa. 43:20b; cf. 41:18; 49:10). The clearest allusion to the Exodus is found in 43:16–19, where Second Isaiah labels the return from exile a "new thing" that is best understood in light of the earlier episode. "Thus says the LORD, who makes a way in the sea, a path in the mighty waters, who brings out chariot and horse, army and warrior; they lie down, they cannot rise, they are extinguished, quenched like a wick: Do not remember the former things, or consider the things of old. I am about to do a new thing; now it springs forth, do you not perceive it? I will make a way in the wilderness and rivers in the desert."

Second Isaiah makes use of the Exodus motif not to trivialize it or downplay its importance—just the opposite. It is such a significant event for the community that it is held up as a model and a lens through which those in exile may interpret their present situation. In this way, the experiences of the present day are put in dialogue with those of people living hundreds of years before.

We began this chapter with a reference to modern music, and that strikes us as a good way to end it. Second Isaiah's method was adopted many centuries later when reggae musician Bob Marley recorded a song titled *Exodus* that appeared on an album of the same name that is generally considered to be one of the greatest albums of the twentieth century. Singing a message of liberation to an audience whose circumstances were similar to, yet different from, those of Second Isaiah, Marley, too, drew upon the traditions of the past. Only this time he had more sources to consult. With a tip of his hat to both the book of Exodus and Second Isaiah, Marley mentions Moses, the Red Sea, and Babylon in his lyrics. And so the cycle of recycling goes on and on.

14

Knowing the Audience

Person to Person

Our era is sometimes referred to as the Communication Age in recognition of the many ways of exchanging information that have emerged and developed in recent decades. Things like cell phones, texting, and e-mail have revolutionized how we relate to one another and keep in touch. Through social networking tools like Facebook, YouTube, and Twitter, people can now open their hearts and bare their souls in living color for the entire world to see. And much of it happens instantaneously. Technological advances now make it possible for someone living in the most remote corner of the world to communicate with people across the planet in the blink of an eye. For example, think about all those communiqués from Osama bin Laden that emanated from Abbottabad, Pakistan, and were broadcast directly into our living rooms.

To refer to our time as the Communication Age doesn't mean people didn't communicate in the past. They did, but it took different forms and usually was much slower. We're both old enough to remember a time when a telephone needed a cord or it wouldn't work. And e-mail? The idea that you could send a written message halfway around the world and have an answer back in minutes was as preposterous as the notion of some television channels broadcasting nothing but news, sports, or comedy twenty-four hours a day. CNN, ESPN, and Comedy Central are proof that miracles do happen, and we can only wonder what amazing forms of communication await humanity in the generations to come.

In the ancient world, as in the modern, a primary means of communicating was via the written word through texts like those that make up the Bible. Some people are not used to thinking about the Bible in this way, but that's exactly what it is—part of the record of communication among people from long ago. Those who consider the Bible to be the word of God often understand the biblical text to be a message direct from God to humanity, literally dictated from on high. But that's not really what the Bible is, or at least not how it was imagined initially. As the material that comprises the Bible was originally written, each author was attempting to communicate to a particular audience. The message might have had something to do with God, or it might have been concerned with something as mundane as a family tree (see Genesis 10, for example).

Over time, through the process of canonization, the Bible took shape and came to be recognized as an authoritative collection of writings for particular groups of people, first Jews and then Christians. At that point, the vertical axis came to dominate and the Bible was understood primarily as the record of God's word to humanity. But it shouldn't be forgotten that the horizontal relationships among people were the starting point for each book that eventually came to be included in the Bible.

If each of the various biblical books was originally intended for a particular audience, then one logical conclusion follows: we're not its original audience and when we read the Bible we are, in effect, reading other people's mail. That doesn't make us the equivalent of cyber thieves who hack their way into someone's e-mail account. We're more like the young kid who eavesdrops on his older sister's phone conversations or reads her diary entries when she's not around, but with an important difference. Little brother never forgets he's not the intended audience of the phone call or diary, and knowing that he isn't is part of the thrill for him. Many Bible readers, though, completely miss the fact that they're reading other people's mail. In the process, they never experience part of the thrill and excitement that comes with being a careful reader of the Bible. We should never forget that the Bible has passed through many hands before reaching our mailbox—in that sense, it's more like chain mail that's forwarded from person to person, generation to generation.

People often assume that the Bible was written for and directed to our day and age, but they're wrong about that. We don't want to be too hard on them, though, because in places the Bible seems to encourage that kind of thinking. The New Testament, for example, often interprets passages from the Hebrew Bible/Old Testament in ways that totally ignore their original context and focus solely on their meaning for a more "modern" audience.

A classic case in point is the way Matthew's Gospel cites passages from the prophets of the Hebrew Bible to explain and interpret various aspects of Jesus' life, a phenomenon discussed in an earlier chapter. One well-known instance is found in Matthew 1:23, which quotes Isaiah 7:14 to support the idea that Jesus was virginally conceived: "Look, the virgin shall conceive and bear a son, and they shall name him Emmanuel." In Isaiah these words are directed to the eighth-century BCE King Ahaz of Judah, who was facing a major international crisis that threatened the survival of his kingdom. The child mentioned in the passage is presented as a sign of hope who would be born during Ahaz's lifetime; there is no hint that it might refer instead to the birth of Jesus, an event that wouldn't take place until more than seven hundred years later. But Matthew's interest is not the original context, and he cites the Isaiah passage as a prediction of Jesus' conception. There's a further problem with this passage in that the Hebrew text of Isaiah doesn't mention a virgin, like the Greek version that Matthew quotes, but we'll save that for another day.

Following a convention that was common at the time, the New Testament contains many examples of similar interpretation of the Hebrew Bible from the perspective of later events, so those who do so in the modern world are in good company. Still, that doesn't make it any less of a problem. We feel that while it's legitimate for later individuals and communities to read the Bible in light of their own circumstances, that approach should never be the starting point. It's important that readers understand as best they can the role a text played in its original context before considering what it might mean for them in theirs.

In this chapter we consider the relationship between biblical texts and their audiences, both original and subsequent. We'll do this through a discussion of apocalyptic literature, one of the most distinctive and unusual styles of writing you'll find in the Bible or anywhere else. The focus will be on the book of Revelation, also known as the Apocalypse, the last book in the Christian canon. We'll also discuss the book of Daniel, the other major example of apocalyptic literature in the Bible.

Because it can be such a perplexing experience, reading apocalyptic literature can sometimes make us aware of the gap between ourselves and its originally intended audience. In other words, here more than anywhere in the Bible we are often conscious that we are reading other people's mail. (And what strange people they are at times!) At the same time, though, there has been a curious tendency on the part of later generations to read and interpret apocalyptic literature, especially Revelation, as if it were speaking directly to them. It therefore serves as a fascinating genre of biblical literature by which to explore the complex relationships that exist between texts and audiences.

It's the End of the World as We Know It

The term *apocalyptic* comes from a Greek word that means "to reveal, unveil," and it describes a type of literature that flourished between the third century BCE and the second century CE. The two biblical books that are representative of the genre are Daniel and Revelation (and not all of Daniel), but there are many examples of Jewish and Christian apocalyptic writing outside the Bible, as well as from other parts of the ancient Near East. Apocalyptic as a literary genre typically takes the form of a message that is sent to a human being through a supernatural intermediary such as an angel. The message describes the transformation of the present world and promises salvation through the defeat of the forces of evil. Apocalyptic writing is often directed to communities that are experiencing crises, and it is meant to instill hope in them and encourage them to remain faithful as they endure their hardships. It offers a word of support that their present situation is not permanent or final and reminds them that God has the last word on how things will turn out.

The opening two verses of the book of Revelation identify it as an apocalyptic work with their reference to a message John received through an angel about future events. "The revelation of Jesus Christ, which God gave him to show his servants what must soon take place; he made it known by sending his angel to his servant John, who testified to the word of God and to the testimony of Jesus Christ, even to all that he saw." It is sometimes claimed that the John mentioned here is also the author of the Gospel that goes by that name, but that idea has been rejected by New Testament scholars. The book of Revelation was probably written sometime in the late first century CE, and all the text tells us about this John is that he was living on the small island of Patmos in the Aegean Sea, probably in exile (1:9).

The first part of the book contains a series of seven messages or letters, each directed to a different church community in Asia Minor. (Talk about reading other people's mail!) They all follow a standard formula that includes an address, a reference to the risen Jesus, words of praise or condemnation for that particular church, a warning, and final words of encouragement for the community of believers. The rest of the book is comprised of a set of strange visions culminating in a battle between the forces of good and evil that ushers in the final age.

The visions contain many unusual elements. The number seven figures prominently in them, and there are references to trumpets, plagues, bowls, and seals (a type of stamp, not the animal). Singing angels fly to and fro, and a slaughtered lamb representing the crucified Jesus makes an appearance (5:1–14). At one point four horses are introduced, each a different color and mounted by a rider who brings punishment and death to the world (6:1–8).

Our fellow sports junkies will be interested to know that the latter scene was the inspiration behind one of the most famous group nicknames in sports history. The starting backfield of the 1924 Notre Dame football team, which went undefeated and was coached by the legendary Knute Rockne, was christened "The Four Horsemen" by the equally legendary sportswriter Grantland Rice. The man knew his Bible. He referred to each of the players in words taken from the book of Revelation. "In dramatic lore their names are Death, Destruction, Pestilence, and Famine. But those are aliases. Their real names are Stuhldreher, Crowley, Miller and Layden." By the way, the rest of their teammates were referred to as "The Seven Mules." We like to think that nickname never caught on in the same way because it had no basis in the Bible.

Various enemies of God populate the pages of Revelation and are referred to as Satan, the Devil, the serpent, the beast, the false prophet, and the whore of Babylon. One by one, they are defeated and overcome by the angelic armies or others acting on behalf of God (17:15–18; 19:11–21; 20:1–3, 7–10). Some of the main themes of the book are found in chapters 12 through 14, which begin with the vision of a pregnant woman who gives birth to a male child but is attacked by a dragon who is identified as Satan. The woman remains unnamed, but in later Christian tradition she is commonly associated with Mary, the mother of Jesus. The archangel Michael and his angels intervene to protect the woman and her son. In chapter 13 the text goes on to describe two beasts who try to deceive humanity to follow them and worship them as gods. This leads to a further set of visions in which angelic messengers attempt to comfort the faithful and convince them to remain true to their beliefs.

The language of apocalyptic literature is sometimes symbolic or metaphorical. We get a good sense of this in the description of the "great whore" in chapter 17. The final verse of the chapter acknowledges the symbolic nature of the description of the woman. "The woman you saw is the great city that rules over the kings of the earth" (17:18). Although she is identified elsewhere in the chapter as Babylon (v. 5), it is generally held that the city being discussed is actually Rome; note that the city sits on seven hills (v. 9). As the Babylonians did in the sixth century CE, the Romans invaded Judah and destroyed the Jerusalem temple in 70 CE, and so the two cities are equated in Revelation. The book's references to the Roman destruction of Jerusalem have played an important role in dating it, with virtually all scholars maintaining that it reached its final form after the year 70.

Symbolism and metaphor continue throughout the chapter. The mention of the woman fornicating with the earth's inhabitants (v. 2) is a comment on Rome's unjust and illegal commercial and political activities. The scarlet beast upon which she sits is the Roman Empire, and its "blasphemous names" are the various divine titles the Roman emperors bestowed upon themselves (v. 3). The woman being drunk with the blood of the saints is an allusion to the suffering and persecution some Christians experienced at the hands of the Roman authorities (v. 6).

It is said about the beast that it "was, and is not, and is about to ascend from the bottomless pit and go to destruction" (v. 8). This is generally considered to be a reference to the emperor Nero, who many believed would come back from death and regain power after his suicide in the year 68. Similarly, the seven kings mentioned in the chapter are commonly understood to be other Roman emperors, some of whom treated Christians harshly.

The climactic scene is found in 19:11–20:15, a section that describes the victory of Christ and his heavenly army over the forces of the beast and the false prophet, who are cast into a fiery lake of burning sulfur (19:11–21). This is followed by the imprisonment of Satan in a pit for one thousand years, during which Christians who were martyred for their faith will be resurrected and rule with Jesus during a period of peace and prosperity. At the end of that time Satan will be set free and wreak havoc on the earth until he is defeated and joins the beast and the false prophet in the fiery lake (20:1–10).

At this point the final judgment takes place as all the dead come before God's throne and are held accountable for their actions. Anyone whose name is not recorded in the book of life is thrown into the lake of fire (20:11–15). Although the location of these events is not specified, it is often identified as Armageddon, a place commonly associated in the popular imagination with a great battle that will take place at the end of time. Its only mention in the Bible is in Revelation 16:16, where it is referred to as "Harmagedon," which is Hebrew for "mount of Megiddo," a city in northern Israel that was located near two major trade routes and was the scene of several important military battles in Israel's history.

At the end of Revelation, John has a vision of a new heaven and a new earth, and an elaborate description is given of a radiantly restored Jerusalem (21:1–22:7). The city no longer needs a temple because God and "the Lamb," meaning Jesus, now occupy it (21:22–23). The forces of evil have been overcome, the world has been radically transformed, and pain, suffering, and death no longer exist (21:3–4).

Are You Talkin' to Me?

As noted earlier, throughout history many people have thought that Revelation provides the key to understanding what's going on in their own day and age. Some have even claimed that the book provides a blueprint for interpreting current events and offers a road map for what lies in the future. In recent times, end-of-the-world scenarios have been popular in films and books like the Left Behind series, and many of these are indebted to Revelation for their ideas and images. People are both fascinated and repulsed by the idea of total annihilation of our planet, and the possibility of such an outcome has become more conceivable in the nuclear age. According to a poll conducted by the Pew Research Center, there are about sixty million evangelicals in the United States and one-third of them think the world will end in their lifetimes. Their religious beliefs and views about the Bible, especially Revelation, are very influential in shaping that belief.

Many of those people are millennialists of one stripe or another. Millennialism is a movement that takes its name from the thousand-year period during which Jesus will reign before the end of the world, according to Revelation. Millennialism interprets literally the book's description of what will occur at the end of time. One of the most famous millennialist groups was the Millerites, an organization founded by William Miller in upstate New York during the nineteenth century that became hugely popular. Basing his calculations on the Bible, particularly the book of Revelation, Miller determined that the world would end sometime between March 21, 1843, and March 21, 1844. At the end of that time period he readjusted the date several times, finally settling on October 22, 1844. When that date passed the group began to splinter and ultimately petered out, eventually morphing into the Seventh Day Adventists.

Belief in the "rapture" is often central to the thought of millennialists and similar groups that anticipate an imminent end to the world. There are various views of what the rapture will entail, but they all agree that upon Jesus' second coming all true believers will be taken from the earth and float up into the air to meet Jesus. This idea is based on a literal reading of 1 Thessalonians 4:15–17, in which Paul speaks of those still living being brought up into the clouds to join Jesus and the deceased. Revelation 4:1 is also sometimes cited in support of the rapture. In that verse John sees an open door in heaven and hears a voice saying, "Come up here, and I will show you what must take place after this." We're not too keen on this type of literal reading of the text, but we do find amusing a phony "story" published in 2001 by a guy named Elroy Willis. It describes the death of a Little Rock woman who leapt through her car's sunroof when she saw some blow-up dolls floating in the air that had escaped from a truck: she mistakenly thought it was the beginning of the rapture. The urban legend went viral on the web and became a huge Internet hit, and also served as the basis for a hilarious episode on the HBO series *Six Feet Under.*

Sometimes such head-in-the-clouds beliefs lead to interpretations that suggest the end-time is just around the corner as disasters, both natural and human-made, are seen to be harbingers of the final days. In the weeks after that tragedy began to unfold, a number of conservative Christian bloggers claimed that the 2010 BP oil spill in the Gulf of Mexico was the fulfillment of Revelation 8:8–9, which describes a burning mountain being thrown into the ocean causing a third of the sea to become blood, a third of sea creatures to die, and a third of the boats to be destroyed. Others have used Revelation to engage in the politics of personal attack. Soon after his election as president, some who disagreed with Barack Obama's policies began to cite the description of the beast in 13:5–8 to argue that he is the antichrist. Actually, the passage is so general and vague that it could have been used by the enemies of any American president in history to smear their foe.

Speaking of individuals whose identities are encoded in Revelation, one of the most discussed passages of the book is the reference to the number of the beast being 666 (13:18). Much ink has been spilled in the quest to decipher the meaning of that enigmatic statement, with various solutions. Most scholars see this as an example of *gematria*, a way of reading that adds up the numerical value of the letters in a word or phrase, and uses that number as a code for the word or phrase. For example, if such a system were applied to English, the number 1 would equal the letter "A," 2 would be "B," and so on. It's the general consensus among Bible scholars that the number 666 is a reference to the Roman Emperor Nero, but that hasn't stopped others from offering all sorts of alternative proposals. Those with anti-Catholic views claim it is a reference to the papacy, while those critical of Islam have seen it as an allusion to the Prophet Muhammad. Other candidates put forward have included Adolph Hitler, Richard Nixon, Saddam Hussein, and Ronald Reagan. If nothing else, such suggestions are a good indication of how some people will go to great lengths to use the Bible in order to support or justify their personal views and agendas.

As we stated earlier, we think it's essential that people understand how Revelation functioned in its original context before they claim it's talking about the BP oil spill, Saddam Hussein, or modern-day helicopters (some people claim that's what the locusts in 9:7–10 actually represent). We, and the rest of the scholarly community with us, don't think the images in the book of Revelation have anything at all to do with contemporary concerns or figures, but if some people choose to believe they do, that's their business. Like most apocalyptic literature, Revelation was written for an audience that was undergoing hardship and was in serious need of support and encouragement. Many New Testament scholars believe it addressed a Christian community that was experiencing suffering and oppression at the hands of a Roman authority that did not share its beliefs, with some suggesting that it was pressuring Christians to reject their faith and embrace the imperial cult. If we're going to apply the book to our own times, maybe that's what we should be focusing on: the context rather than the content. Instead of adopting a literal reading of the text that tries to match every item with a corresponding element in our time, we should read it for the lessons it might be able to teach us about how to respond to the modern forms of temptation, evil, and injustice that we confront on a daily basis. Apocalyptic writing is ultimately about the transformation of the world through the removal of those things that perpetuate inequality and intolerance. That's precisely where the modern-day relevance of the book can be found. We would be truer to John of Patmos and his vision if we were to ask how we might go about that transformative task and create our own vision of a better world.

Daniel

The other major example of apocalyptic writing in the Bible is found in the second half of the book of Daniel. The book of Daniel is set in Babylon during the sixth century BCE, but was probably written much later. The opening chapters tell of the experiences and adventures of Daniel and other young Israelites who served as attendants to the Babylonian king Nebuchadnezzar. These stories are in the form of court tales, and they include some famous biblical passages, like the account of how Daniel's three friends survived being thrown into a fiery furnace (ch. 3) and the description of how Daniel managed to spend an entire night in a den of lions without being harmed (ch. 6).

With chapter 7 the genre of the book dramatically changes, and its second half is mainly comprised of three visions. There are two brief visions in chapters 7 and 8, and a longer one in chapters 10 through 12. Most of the ninth chapter is a prayer of confession for Israel's sins. All three visions tell about the rise of an oppressive ruler who will eventually be overthrown by God. The two halves of the book are therefore quite distinct and most likely were originally independent. Further complicating the question of the origin of the material in Daniel is the fact that the language of the text changes from Hebrew to Aramaic in 2:4b and doesn't revert back to Hebrew until the beginning of the eighth chapter. The Aramaic section therefore bridges the genre shift from nonapocalyptic to apocalyptic writing. The use of different languages is evidence of the growth and development of the book. Many scholars believe that chapters 8–12 were the last section of the book to be written and that 1:1–2:4a was added to provide an introductory frame for the Aramaic section.

The second half of Daniel exhibits many of the features we've already noted in Revelation. Daniel is incapable of understanding the meanings of the visions, and so he must rely on supernatural intermediaries to explain their significance. Each vision describes the transformation of the present world through the defeat of evil, and promises salvation for those who remain faithful until the end. Like its New Testament counterpart, the Apocalypse, Daniel is chock-full of symbolism referring to historical events and figures that must be decoded in order to understand the message.

As with Revelation and other apocalyptic writings, Daniel was written to a community that was experiencing persecution and hardship, only in this case it was at the hands of the Greeks rather than the Romans. Filling in for Nero is Antiochus IV Epiphanes, a nasty tyrant whose invasion of Jerusalem in 167 BCE began a reign of terror. He killed many of the city's inhabitants, forbade Jews from practicing their faith, and even erected an altar dedicated to Zeus in the temple, upon which he allegedly sacrificed a pig. Antiochus's campaign to suppress Judaism created a hostile environment that put Jews at great risk and caused many to reconsider their religious commitments. Historical clues in the book suggest that the apocalyptic portion of Daniel addresses this situation and encourages Jews to remain faithful by envisioning the downfall of Antiochus and the reward that awaits those who do not give in to him.

To illustrate how this works, we'll briefly consider the vision in chapter 7. It begins with Daniel seeing four beasts, which a heavenly attendant explains to him represent four kingdoms (vv. 15–17). These kingdoms are generally held to be Babylon, Media, Persia, and Greece. The fourth beast (Greece) is the most terrifying and different from the others in that it has ten horns. As Daniel observes the horns, another one appears that has human eyes, speaks arrogantly, and makes war against the holy ones (vv. 7–8, 21). His interpreter informs Daniel that the ten horns represent ten kings, and the eleventh one is another ruler who will blaspheme God, persecute believers, and have no regard for religious observances. "He shall speak words against the Most High, shall wear out the holy ones of the Most High, and shall attempt to change the sacred seasons and the law" (v. 25). That is to say, this horn symbolizes Antiochus and his brutal treatment of the Jews. But the messenger assures Daniel that the little horn will be destroyed and the holy ones who remain faithful will be rewarded (vv. 26–27).

The other two visions differ in the details, but follow the general outline of the first one by symbolically presenting Antiochus as the latest of the Greek rulers who is antagonistic toward God's people but who will eventually be overcome. In several places his desecration of the Jerusalem Temple is mentioned (8:11–12; 11:31).

What's really interesting about the way the book presents these visions is that it gives the impression that they are predictions of future events by locating Daniel in Babylon during the sixth century BCE, long before the rise of Greece and the coming of Antiochus IV Epiphanes. In fact, there's a bit of sleight of hand going on here because the book was actually written in the second century BCE and the events that are being "predicted" have already happened. The term sometimes used for this is *vaticinium ex eventu*, Latin for "prediction after the event."

The clearest indication that the book comes from the second century BCE rather than the sixth is the way it treats Antiochus's death. The long vision in chapters 10 through 12 contains references to various episodes in Antiochus's reign, and in each case these correspond to historical details that can be documented from extrabiblical sources. But the vision gets things wrong in the description of his death in 11:45. The text says that he will conquer Egypt and his end will come when he returns to Judah and sets up his war-tent between Jerusalem and the Mediterranean. In fact, Antiochus never defeated Egypt and he died in Persia while on a military campaign. From this we may infer that Antiochus's death had not yet occurred at the time the book was written, and the author was going out on a limb by anticipating the type of death he would have.

Presenting the message in this way must have had a powerful rhetorical effect on its original second-century BCE audience. From their perspective the events in Daniel's sixth-century visions had all come to pass. If he were a baseball player, he'd be batting 1.000. We can imagine them thinking, "If the visions Daniel had four hundred years earlier predicted the events of our own day so perfectly, then surely what he saw regarding our future must be accurate, too. That bully Antiochus's days are numbered, so all we have to do is remain faithful and everything will turn out okay." It's a foolproof way of persuading people to accept your argument or "prediction."

But just for good measure in 12:2 the author offers a carrot on a stick meant to address anyone who's on the fence. "Many of those who sleep in the dust of the earth shall awake, some to everlasting life, and some to shame and everlasting contempt." This is arguably the Hebrew Bible's only reference to resurrection of the dead. The message it delivers to Daniel's audience is unmistakable: you had better remain faithful and not be swayed by Antiochus and those like him or you will suffer serious and eternal consequences. That should keep them on the straight and narrow. We'd be remiss if we didn't point out how late the belief in life after death enters the biblical literature. Prior to the second century BCE there's no clear evidence for something that most Jews and Christians consider to be a foundation of their faiths. Many scholars think the idea may have been introduced from Babylon during the exilic period or through Greek thought, ironically the very places Daniel warns his readers about.

This chapter has discussed the only two clear-cut representatives of apocalyptic writing that we have in the Bible. Some have argued that elements of apocalyptic can be found in other books like Ezekiel and Isaiah, especially in chapters 24–27 of the latter. That may be so, but it would be an exaggeration to call them full-blown examples of the apocalyptic genre. We've focused on the importance of understanding the context of its original audience to have a proper understanding of an apocalyptic work's meaning and purpose. While Daniel is less commonly misread in that fashion, our treatment of Revelation highlighted the problems that can result from ignoring an apocalyptic book's original context and simply applying it directly to our own times. The same might be said about any passage in the Bible. We should never forget that the pieces of mail that comprise the text were meant for other hands and have been forwarded to us.

ADDITIONAL RESOURCES

Beal, Timothy. *The Rise and Fall of the Bible: The Unexpected History of an Accidental Book*. New York: Houghton Mifflin Harcourt, 2011.

Borowski, Oded. *Daily Life in Biblical Times*. Atlanta: Society of Biblical Literature, 2003.

Brown, Raymond E., Joseph A. Fitzmyer, and Roland E. Murphy, eds. *The New Jerome Biblical Commentary*. Upper Saddle River, NJ: Prentice Hall, 1999.

Curtis, Adrian. *Oxford Bible Atlas*. 4th ed. New York: Oxford University Press, 2009.

Kaltner, John, Steven L. McKenzie, and Joel Kilpatrick. *The Uncensored Bible: The Bawdy and Naughty Bits of the Good Book*. San Francisco: HarperOne, 2008.

King, Philip J., and Lawrence E. Stager. *Life in Biblical Israel*. Louisville, KY: Westminster John Knox Press, 2002.

Matthews, Victor H. *Manners and Customs in the Bible*. Peabody, MA: Hendrickson Publishers, 1991.

McKenzie, Steven L., and Stephen R. Haynes, eds. *To Each Its Own Meaning: Biblical Criticisms and Their Applications*. Rev. ed. Louisville, KY: Westminster John Knox Press, 1999.

McKenzie, Steven L., and John Kaltner. *The Old Testament: Its Background, Growth, and Content*. Nashville: Abingdon Press, 2007.

Metzger, Bruce M. *The New Testament: Its Background, Growth, and Content*. 3rd ed. Nashville: Abingdon Press, 2003.

Metzger, Bruce M., and Michael D. Coogan, eds. *The Oxford Companion to the Bible*. 3rd ed. New York: Oxford University Press, 1993.